AF248814

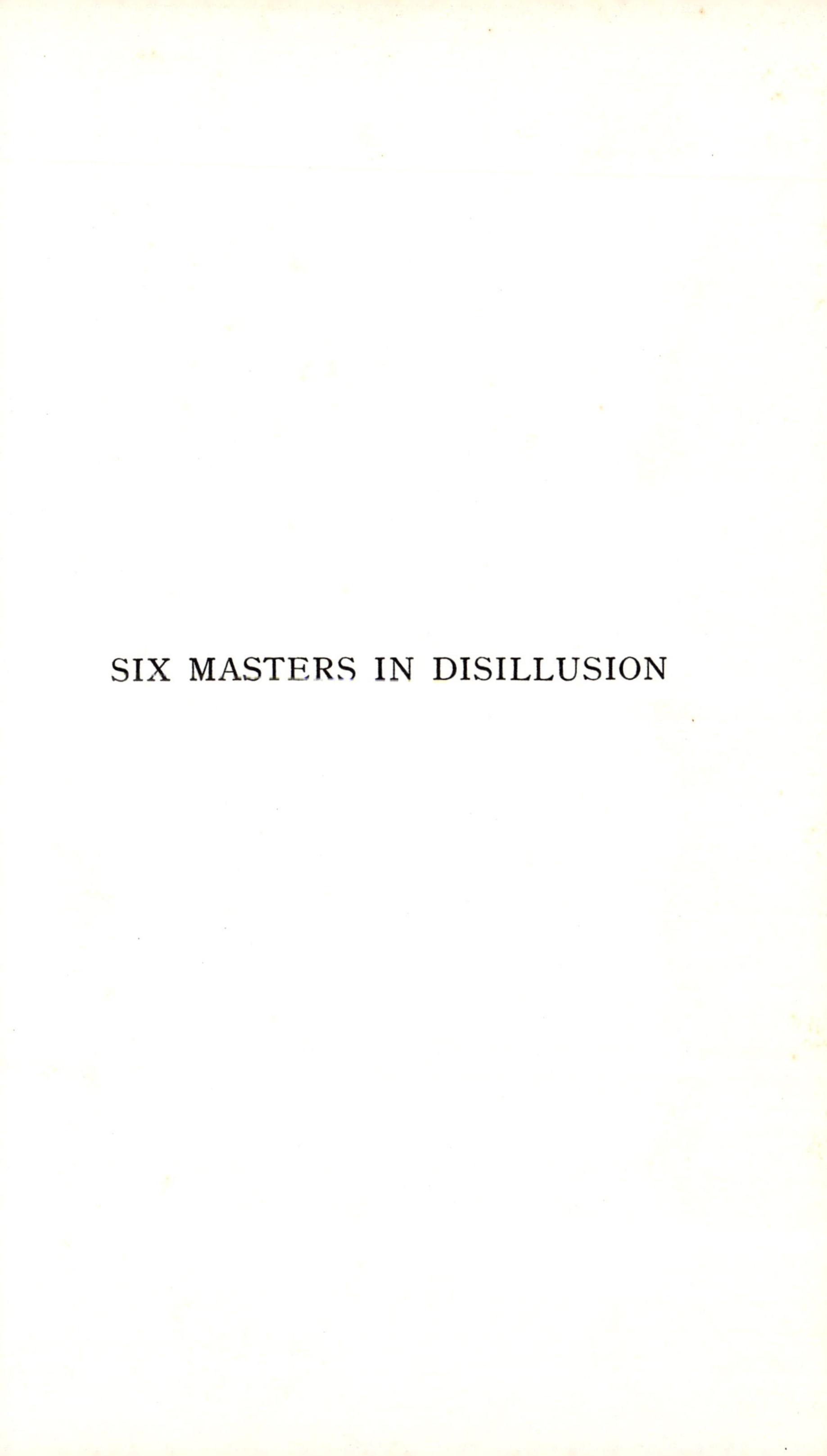

SIX MASTERS IN DISILLUSION

SIX MASTERS IN DISILLUSION

BY

ALGAR THOROLD

KENNIKAT PRESS
Port Washington, N. Y./London

SIX MASTERS IN DISILLUSION

First published in 1909
Reissued in 1971 by Kennikat Press
Library of Congress Catalog Card No: 75-113325
ISBN 0-8046-1364-8

Manufactured by Taylor Publishing Company Dallas, Texas

TO THE READER

In order that the reader may be as little disappointed as possible with these studies, I must explain that they are not concerned with strictly contemporary disillusion. The period which they are intended, in a very partial and tentative way, to illustrate is behind us, and its forces are in great measure already spent. Contemporary disillusion, of which, among the writers here noticed, Anatole France alone could fairly be considered an example, is a different matter. Our fathers were rationalists, and were naïve enough to think that Theology stood or fell by its claims to rationality. They thought that the cosmology and psychology of Christianity, the propositions which it enunciated about the nature of man and the world he finds himself in, were intended to be taken as facts. As facts they tested them, with the result that the account of the world and man contained in the

Sacred Books of Christianity and the authoritative decrees of the Church, have ceased to form part of the mental culture of the West-European races. For although the Catholic Church still lives—and he must know little of humanity who doubts that it will go on living—ecclesiastical cosmology, history and psychology are things of the past as irrelevant to contemporary knowledge as the Hindu Pantheon or Muslim Demonology. The work of the rationalist emancipators in this respect has been done, and done so thoroughly that it forms part of the unquestioned mental heritage that everybody takes for granted. Nevertheless we, or at least those of us who are disillusioned to-day, are not rationalists. We have pushed analysis further than our fathers did, nay, in our turn, we have laid sacrilegious hands on their standard of truth. It has fared no better at our hands than that of their fathers did at theirs. This is, however, not the place to discuss contemporary disillusion.

It is in the disillusionment consequent on this change of attitude towards Christianity in which the writers studied here agree. In nearly everything else they differ. Fontenelle, a sort of smiling malicious Precursor of the Evangel of the last two centuries, seems to attain prophetically the scepticism of a later period. He was a very difficult person to pay with words. Mérimée, equally detached from the optimism of the eighteenth century, presents rather the elegant cynicism of the man of the world who will not admit that he is wounded to the heart. The masterly studies of ecclesiastical psychology which we owe to Ferdinand Fabre indicate one aspect of the line of defence adopted by the clergy against the changed world in which they find themselves. That attitude was an important factor in the politics of every country in Europe where the Church had power during the nineteenth century, and contributed most effectively to the detachment of the educated classes from Christianity. Maeterlinck, on the other hand, while emphatically post-Christian, and therefore deriving from the specific disillusionment of the eighteenth century, retains much of the optimism of the Fathers of the Encyclopædia. Indeed his optimism is but faintly tempered by the delays and incertitudes of science, not at all by philosophical analysis, while his appreciation of the enormous difficulties in the way of any serious human advance, his view of the actual situation, seem at times disconcertingly vague. But then he has the divine gift of mysticism, a very special mysticism of his own, if you will, inspired, in so far as it is philosophical, by Hartmann's 'Unconscious,' made effective through the essential poetry of his own nature.

Anatole France, as I have said, represents a riper mood of scepticism, the mood of Renan in his last years. The vision of the age of reason which inspires the labours of the Encyclopædists no longer inspires him. In him disillusion may be said to reach its term. Yet, in many ways, he is the most *dix-huitième* of any writer of the present time. The optimism, which, as far as rational tests go, is in no better position than theology, has nevertheless left in his mind a sweet and mellow compassion for humanity, an inextinguishable love of man, which gives an irresistible attractiveness to his work at its best, and then his exquisite manner, the naïve charm with which he presents his purely intellectual perversity recalls so delightfully the *mignardise* of the age of salons.

Among these writers perhaps the most bitter and poignant master in disillusion is Huysmans. Disillusion does not remain a purely intellectual phase, and no one has expressed more vividly than he, its sentimental and sensuous reactions. The course which his personal disillusion among other motives led him to adopt, while itself obviously outside legitimate criticism, serves nevertheless as the measure of the depth to which that disillusion went.

CONTENTS

PAGE

TO THE READER, ... v

FONTENELLE, ... 1

PROSPER MÉRIMÉE, ... 26

FERDINAND FABRE, ... 56

JORIS-KARL HUYSMANS, ... 80

MAETERLINCK, ... 96

ANATOLE FRANCE, ... 119

EPILOGUE, ... 147

ERRATA

P. 84, line 4. *For* 'absent from the pages' *read* 'absent from these pages.'

P. 87, line 14. *For* 'hence the success of the uneducated' *read* 'hence her success with the uneducated.'

P. 91, line 8. *For* 'qu'il semble une parole, issue de l'accouplement de Lisa' *read* 'qu'il semble, ma parole, issu de l'accouplement de Lisa.'

P. 116, line 8. *For* 'The generalisations by means of which we organise what we call "external,"' *read* 'The generalisations by means of which we organise what we call "external reality."'

FONTENELLE

THE extraordinary clear-headedness of the French, their readiness to pursue an idea to its logical term and its complete literary and social expression, gives to their fortunes at any given moment, an air of finality which seems at first sight to contradict that law of perpetual variation, which we know to reign in the process of human affairs, as in all other manifestations of Nature. It is needless to say that this appearance is delusive; changes occur in France as elsewhere. And, owing perhaps to this very capacity for logic in the French, they occur there in the most startling and dramatic way: generally in the way of a complete *volte-face*; all must be pulled down, all must be built anew. Napoleon has hardly climbed to the height of his uncertain despotism, when he proceeds to remodel the whole religious and social life of the nation, as if he were founding an empire for eternity, instead of for eleven years. He falls, and Monarchy and Republic follow each other with bewildering rapidity. Nevertheless below the surface, scintillating with *coups d'État* and proclamations, appeals to the people and counter-proclamations, all based on mutually exclusive first principles, the work of slow and gradual transition goes on. The character of an individual does not move as quickly as his mere intellect: still more uneven in their gait are mental and temperamental changes in a nation. This law of variability, the condition of all life, was never more completely ignored than in the France of the seventeenth century. All then was built for eternity, and seemed, indeed, in a fair way to possess it. The great *châteaux* of the period, some of which, spared by the Revolution, still stand as symbols of that brilliant past, did not defy the hand of time more audaciously than the theories of its philosophers, theologians and politicians. They were more successful in their defiance, because masonry, if good enough, enjoys a permanence denied to systems of thought. From the great King himself—one of the few kings who have also been statesmen—down to the lay-sisters of Port Royal, all, whether their cause were the political greatness of the nation, the superiority of the Ancients over the Moderns, or the niceties of prevenient Grace, fought in it from the point of view which may be supposed to animate St. Michael in his contest with Lucifer. Truth was absolute, Truth was eternal, error must, in the long run, fail from a sort of metaphysical necessity. It was but a dream, though a great and majestic one, and France has not yet got through the throes of her awakening. Nevertheless some of the acutest intellects that have ever been, took it for a reality. Let us humble ourselves.

There could be no greater mistake than to imagine that the affirmations of the seventeenth century in thought, in theology, in statecraft, were but vain forms of words, idly repeated by a generation which had no taste for speculative inquiry. On the contrary, that century was a far more truly philosophical period than the succeeding one which usurped the name. Pascal, the Prometheus of modern Catholicism, stands alone in the magnificence of his despair, Descartes and Malebranche are the two French philosophers who have a real claim to be considered metaphysicians. The genius of the age was constructive in every department of human affairs. It was constructive, and it undertook its task in an *a priori* spirit. Every one argued from absolute premisses to irrefragable conclusions. It was not only the party in authority that did so; Jurieu treated the recalcitrant Bayle in precisely the same way as he himself had been treated by Bossuet. It did not occur to any one to appeal to facts, partly because most of the controversies in the air could hardly be affected by such an appeal, and partly because men had hardly come to recognise their relevance to their own well-being. Yet, just then, unsuspected by philosophers and theologians, after an interval of centuries, during which men had a free hand with which to fashion a cosmos in their own image, the Fact was being born again into the world of human significance. It was their unconsciousness of this which delivered these great thinkers bound into the hands of their successors of the following century, men as a rule considerably their inferiors, both in intellect and imagination. Already when the glory of Lewis the Great was at its height, when Bossuet's *Universal History* appeared to culminate, and thereby find its justification in the Church and State of France, the man was born who represented in his life and work, more completely perhaps than any contemporary, the coming spirit of negation and criticism which was surely to sap the foundations of that splendid edifice. That man was Fontenelle.

Bernard le Bovier, Sieur de Fontenelle, was born at Rouen in 1657. It was one of his originalities to live to be a centenarian, an originality which enabled him to fill successively the rôles of prophet and traditional authority. To the seventeenth century he prophesied of what was to come, and to the eighteenth he stood as a reminder of its origins. No one contributed more than he did to the bringing about of that vast change in opinion which occurred during his lifetime.

The right view of Fontenelle is not quite easy. No one was ever less like an apostle of new and unwelcome truths. He was the first specimen of a new race of writers. He wrote poetry without being a poet, philosophy without being a philosopher, science without being an experimentalist. He does not appear to have had a passion for truth, but, on the whole, to have preferred it; the gossip of his time reflects him as moved by a tempered curiosity, mitigated by a love of ease and good food. Voltaire, whose enthusiasm could hardly brook so measured a zeal, summed him up, not without a touch of malice, as 'le discret Fontenelle.' His bonne amie, Mme. du Tencin, placing her hand on his heart one day, said to him: '*Vous n'avez là que du cerveau.*' Although he allowed Mme. de Lambert to be his almoner, he appeared to pride himself on his egotism. To him is attributed the well-known recipe for happiness—*tenir le cœur froid et l'estomac chaud.* He may have thought it, but it would hardly have been in keeping with his discretion to have said so. His wit was inimitable. An aged lady having one day said to him: 'It seems that Providence has forgotten us on this earth,' 'Chut, on pourra nous entendre,' replied Fontenelle, placing his finger on his mouth with an air of mystery. His main characteristic was moderation in all things, a moderation which evidently must have been based on singularly torpid senses. Mme. Geoffrin tells us that he never laughed or wept, he was never in a hurry, and never even approximated to losing his temper. When he took an apartment he left the furniture exactly as he found it, without changing a nail. Most wonderful of all, when he had gout, it was painless; 'seulement son pied devenait du coton, il le posait sur un fauteuil, et c'était tout.'

Before proceeding to the part he played in forming his age, it will be useful to consider, rather more in detail, the nature of that great change in human opinion to which I have already referred, and which marks off the eighteenth from the preceding century. Bossuet gave to the absolutism, both civil and ecclesiastical, of his time a final and classical expression; in order, then, to know what it was that the eighteenth century superseded, it is to Bossuet that we must go. One of the clearest heads and greatest masters of style that ever lived, he never leaves us in any doubt as to his meaning. 'If,' says Sir James Stephen, 'it were the order of nature that God should be represented upon earth by infallible priests and irresponsible kings, it would be impossible to imagine a nobler system of education for a great king than that which Bossuet conceived, or a teacher better suited to carry it out than Bossuet himself.' The education of the ill-fated dauphin furnished him with the occasion for the expression of his theory of human life. The *Connaissance de Dieu et de Soi-même*, the *Discours sur l'Histoire Universelle*, and the *Politique tirée de l'Ecriture Sainte*, were the three divisions into which his teaching naturally fell, and these books remain for ever among the finest examples of the constructive power of human genius and the most important landmarks in the history of European thought. Their rhetoric is so ample and so magnificent, their reasoning so close and so solid, that even now one is tempted to overlook the baselessness of their premisses, and can hardly believe that so substantial-seeming a fabric melts under criticism into 'air, thin air,' with all 'the cloud-capped towers, the gorgeous palaces, the solemn temples' of its visionary splendour.

Renan has told us that the mediæval scholastic was, in spite of his mysticism, a sound rationalist, *i.e.* he accepted the fact of revelation as the ultimate term of a process of reasoning which started from grounds level with the rest of experience, and that it was not until such grounds had given way, that ecclesiastical apologists were driven to 'prove the divinity of Jesus Christ by the battle of Marengo.'

Bossuet would have shared Renan's contempt for the modern apologists of 'Fideism.' It certainly would be hard to find in Voltaire or in Tom Paine a more uncompromising expression of the principles of the early rationalists than the following little piece of epistemology which occurs in the *De la Connaissance de Dieu et de Soi-même.* 'The understanding (l'entendement) is the light which God has given us for our guidance. It has different names; in its inventive and penetrating capacity it is called spirit (esprit): in so far as it judges and directs to truth and goodness, it is called reason and judgment. Reason, in so far as it turns us from the true evil of man, which is sin, is called conscience.' And he says that reason, if not seduced by passion, is infallible. 'The understanding is never forced to err, and never does so *except from want of attention: and if it judges wrongly by following the senses or passions derived from them too readily, it will correct its judgment if a right will make it attentive to its object and itself.*' (The italics are mine.) Certainly Bossuet cannot be said to err in putting the power of reason too low. What was it, then, he lacked? He lacked facts, or rather he took for facts what were not facts, and the reason he did so was that he had no criticism. His superb eloquence and the rationalism of his process blinded him to the sources of his premisses, which were, in truth, his conclusions. He somewhat naïvely betrays himself in his controversy with Richard Simon, the Oratorian father, who, two centuries before Loisy, maintained in the Catholic Church the right of reason to investigate the title-deeds of theology. '*Les dates font tout en ces matières!*' he cries. Yes, indeed. All the more reason, one would think, to subject them to the severest scrutiny. Let us, however, not be unjust. It would be idle and absurd to blame Bossuet for his lack of acquaintance with the science of historical criticism; it is not illegitimate to deplore the spirit of blind certitude which prevented him understanding the nature and relevance of Père Simon's inquiries. He seems to have regarded such speculations from that purely conventional and professional point of view which the more educated Christian pulpit of to-day, whether Catholic or Protestant, does not hesitate to disavow. The view which Bossuet derived from, among others, 'quatre ou cinq faits authentiques et plus clairs que la lumière du soleil (qui) font voir notre religion aussi ancienne que le monde'—one gasps at the statement—was one of the most complete and universal absolutism. Whatever might be said about nature, it was indeed the divine order 'that God should be represented upon earth by infallible priests and irresponsible kings.' And the chain of such representatives had never been broken. 'From Innocent XI., who fills to-day so worthily the first place in the Church,' he traces back that august line through St. Peter and the Pontiffs of the ancient Law to Moses and Aaron: 'de là jusqu'à l'origine du monde! quelle suite, quelle tradition, quel enseignement merveilleux!' One is reminded of Pascal's 'Sem qui a vu Lamech, qui a vu Adam, a vu aussi Jacob qui a vu ceux qui ont vu Moïse. Donc le déluge et la création sont vrais.' Certainly Bossuet was right, as a matter of tactics, in resenting criticism of the Mosaic authorship of the Pentateuch. He was right, that is to say, so long as it was possible to suppress such criticism by other than critical methods: but although he knew it not, the day of such absolute power, whether in the realm of opinion or politics, was drawing to its close. And now we may return to the part played by Fontenelle in the transition.

What that transition led to primarily was the emancipation of the individual judgment from the control of authority of any kind. This emancipation constituted the first 'moment' of modern rationalism. In that moment the individual was conceived as self-subsisting, infallible in his understanding (to which understanding, precisely reproduced in every human being, 'Reality' was exactly correlative), and perfect in will, *i.e.* spontaneously and naturally good. Ignorance and sin, moral and intellectual evil, were brought about by the environment of humanity, and were due to the institutions which prevented man's understanding and will having free play. Taken as a whole and in its maturity this attitude represents the most naïve and simple form of individualistic optimism. Its philosopher was Voltaire and its religion was Deism; and the French Revolution and Kant were lying in wait for it. Though the apprehensions on which the movement was based were essentially positive, its first attitude was inevitably one of negation—negation of the values enshrined in the system with which it found itself in conflict. That system, as we have seen, held the whole of human life in the meshes of authority; the first task of the emancipators was then to dislodge authority. Until that was done nothing could be done. Now the phenomenal basis of the Church's authority was as such, unsound, for the facts on which it was alleged to rest could not be proved. Bossuet's line of communication between Heaven and Earth was discovered, on investigation, to be non-existent. This was the position of the early rationalists, and so far they were right, and, as long as the Church confined her apologetics to mere empiricism, she was bound to be beaten, for she was not so good an empiricist as the *philosophes*. When, however, from being negative, they became positive, and took over human nature themselves on the schematism of the authority of the understanding, relying on the formal contraries of the Church's ethical teaching, on *i.e.* the natural rectitude of each human will as such, and on the perfectibility, in terms of present experience, of humanity considered as an aggregate of individuals, they failed. Kant blew up their naïve objectivism, showed that the Deistic God who was conceived as a part only of all reality was a mass of contradictions insoluble to the individual understanding, while the Revolution and its resulting reactions gave pause to their social speculations. So it comes about that the name of a pioneer of the movement like Fontenelle is mainly associated with rebellion against the Church. M. Faguet has severely criticised his methods. I would suggest in deprecation of his criticism that it cannot have been very easy at the time to see how such an attack could be led. For although ecclesiastical authority could not, in strict logic and theology, have axiomatic value, for its existence was given as a phenomenal fact, based like others on evidence, appealing finally to the individual judgment, yet in process of time it had naturally enough come to have some such value for its adherents. And, at the time of which I am writing, only very few French men or women were not its adherents. Moreover, on the Catholic premisses, the moral values of life were inextricably intertwined with the assents of Faith : it was impossible to prove the purity of the motives which led to their rejection. If the orthodox were unable to impute that favourite commonplace of the controversial pulpit, a desire for sensual indulgence, to the Freethinkers, they could always fall back upon pride, an absolutely unanswerable charge. Also it must be remembered that although Louis XIV had refused, at the time of the Revocation of the Edict of Nantes, to re-establish the suppressed Inquisition, the Parliament of Paris did not scruple to use force in defence of orthodoxy. All this rendered necessary, or appeared to render necessary, to the great men who began the emancipation of the French mind, a course of systematic concealment of the real extent of their dissent from the popular creed, which, in our own day, would be repugnant, it may be hoped, to both the defenders and the opponents of any established form of Christianity.

It is impossible to deny that Fontenelle had a natural aptitude for the part. Indeed, so admirably fitted was he for it that, on the providential theory of the apparition of great men, such a coincidence between the workman and the task seems to speak incontrovertibly in favour of a special design. To say as much as this is to admit that Fontenelle's character leaves much to be desired: I have already pointed out that it was not through the individual superiority of their champions that the ideas of the eighteenth century succeeded in replacing those of the preceding one. It was the stars in their courses that fought for them, the process of nature, the unconscious dialectic of things, that was their secret accomplice.

Fontenelle's first appearance in literature, apart from his share in the quarrel of the Ancients and the Moderns, with which we are here hardly concerned, was, oddly enough, as a poet. It has been ingeniously remarked that while his ideas were in advance of his time, his style was behind it. This is true of his poetry at least. His *Pastorales*, his *Bergeries* and his *Églogues* are pure Louis XIII. Inane and insipid as they are, they are, however, without the note of falseness characteristic of the *genre*. His shepherds do not talk like poets and philosophers, and he cleverly avoids the snare of the literary convention of rusticity. This is something to be thankful for, but not to be false is not enough for art. His Coryns and Phebes are pure nullities. They simply do not exist at all. In his *Discours sur la nature de l'Églogue* he naïvely remarks: 'La poésie pastorale n'a pas grand charme si elle ne roule que sur les choses de la campagne. Entendre parler de brebis et de chèvres cela n'a rien par soi-même qui puisse plaire.' The opinion is defensible, but seems out of place on the lips of a pastoral poet. He appears to have seen only one thing in the 'simple life,' namely leisure, and judges, in his dispassionate way, that this would probably lead to an unusual development of amativeness. So he gives us scenes of a cool and measured gallantry, in which neither his own nor his reader's interest is ever for a moment seriously engaged. One imagines him reading them aloud to Mme. du Tencin or Mme. de Lambert, punctuated by the handling of his snuff-box, and an occasional drawing-room smirk. Truly, '*C'est une chose d'une tristesse morne, que les juvenilia d'un homme qui n'a jamais eu de jeunesse.*' It is unnecessary even to mention his tragedies, which are the productions, says M. Faguet, of a man who is the nephew of Corneille, but who appears to be his uncle. Fontenelle was clever enough to realise in time that he had mistaken his vocation. Perhaps it came home to him when he was correcting the proofs of his fourth Eclogue, in which occurs what is surely the most unpoetical line ever written in metre:

> 'Quand on a le cœur tendre, il ne faut pas qu'on aime.'

La Bruyère, who hated him, gave him a place

among his 'Caractères' as Cydias. 'Cydias (est) bel esprit : c'est sa profession. Il a une enseigne, un atelier, des ouvrages de commande, et des compagnes qui travaille sous lui. Prose, vers, que voulez-vous ? il réussit également en l'un et en l'autre. Demandez-lui des lettres de consolation, ou sur une absence, il les entreprendra ; prenez les toutes faites et entrez dans son magasin, il y a à choisir.' There is this amount of truth under La Bruyère's rather savage attack, that Fontenelle, while entirely devoid of enthusiasm, except on one subject which we will shortly consider, possessed so supple a brain as to produce the effect of a universal intelligence. As a poet he failed, nor need his failure surprise us, for more than a supple brain is required for the production of poetry. The fact is that he was a characteristic and magnificent man of letters, being, indeed, the first specimen of that type which was to play so important a part throughout the eighteenth century. Now the man of letters, as such, does not need to be an original thinker, still less need he be a creative artist. On the other hand he requires, in order to fulfil his functions in the republic of the mind, a quick and facile intelligence, apt to seize the finer shades of opinion, all of which he should be ready to welcome in turn. For he must be without prejudices of any kind, which, in the average state of human nature, is tantamount to saying he must eschew personal convictions. He is skilled to detect the real trend of ideas; among contemporary notions he readily, and, as it were, instinctively, distinguishes those that are pregnant with the future from merely associational survivals. He is to the thinkers who are the creative forces of the time, what the *Pensée*-writer is to the moral philosopher, he circulates the small change of their ideas. He can only permit himself one passion, curiosity: but the more he has of that the better. Fontenelle was all this in a supreme degree. I have said that he had one enthusiasm. There was one thing in which that *dilettante,* indifferent spirit really did believe, and that one thing was science. Here he showed the *flair* of the perfect man of letters, in recognising, almost at its birth, the new energy which was to play such a part in the immediate future, while, at the same time, he gratified his curiosity, the most fundamental and serious tendency of his nature. Already, in 1680, when St. Simon had set the fashion to the Court of an occasional retreat in the austere cloisters of de Rancé, Fontenelle was in the habit of disappearing for several days at a time. He was not at La Trappe, but in a little house in the Faubourg St. Jacques. Here he used to meet and confer with the mathematician Varignon, the Abbé de St.

Pierre, and other scientific persons. This little house was, indeed, the cradle of the eighteenth century in France. If Bayle provided in his dictionary an arsenal of sceptical arguments for the *philosophes* to direct against the Church, it was from the *cénacle* of the Faubourg St. Jacques that the positive side of the movement proceeded. That positive side aimed at what all the scepticism in the world never could have effected, the substitution of the prestige of science for that of the Church. It is often said that Fontenelle, unlike those robust dogmatists who carried the movement which he had helped to initiate to its maturity, was a sceptic. It is very much a question of words. All who question the values of popular theology or politics are apt to incur the charge. For it is the nature of those values to be held by those who maintain them with such immediacy of conviction that discussion of any kind is apt to seem an irrelevant impertinence, more or less certainly of the nature of doubt. I do not think that Fontenelle was in doubt on the subject of Christian theology, as the tradition of the Church of his day presented it. In spite of his cautious mode of expression, of the modesty—or diplomacy — with which he refrained from pushing his arguments to their legitimate conclusion, from committing himself to an open breach with ecclesiastical authority, there is, I think, no sort of doubt that he positively, and with full conviction, rejected the whole system. The Fathers of the Society of Jesus, who are not supposed to be particularly stupid people, were quick to detect the 'essential impiety' of his *Histoire des Oracles*, which is, ostensibly, a defence of pure religion from the ill-informed zeal of its misguided advocates. Nay, we must go further. Not only do I think that Fontenelle was definitely anti-Christian, but it seems unquestionable that his mind, his temperament, his character, call it what you will, was incurably hostile to religion of any kind. He did not accept the Church's Messiah, and felt no sort of necessity to look for another. The good Fathers were right, his impiety was essential. To slightly alter a well-known ecclesiastical formula, he may be said to have been invincibly irreligious. This appears I think very clearly in his *Entretiens sur la Pluralité des Mondes*, which is interesting as being one of the first attempts at the popularisation of science. It was published in 1686. Fontenelle says in the preface that he asks the same attention from ladies in order to understand all he has to tell them—'tout ce système de philosophie'—as is required to enjoy the *Princesse de Clèves*. And so clear is his exposition, that his astronomy reads like a novel. The book had an immediate and immense success. *Toutes ces dames* devoured it eagerly, which shows the ground covered in fifteen years since the publication of the *Femmes Savantes.* In 1671 the *Entretiens* would have died of ridicule. The form is very characteristic. The astronomer shows the heavens at night to a charming marquise, whose questions and comments enable him to relieve the strain of the reader's attention, by neatly turned compliments and gallant epigrams. The marquise having remarked that the beauty of the day is that of a brilliant blonde, while the beauty of the night possesses the more touching quality of the brunette, her instructor replies: 'J'en conviens: mais en récompense une blonde comme vous me ferait encore mieux rêver que la plus belle nuit du monde avec toute sa beauté brune.' The little book is not, however, made up of such courtly trifling. It goes far, very far. 'Il serait embarassant en théologie qu'il y eût des hommes qui ne descendissent point d'Adam . . . mais je ne mets dans la lune que des habitants qui ne sont point des hommes.' A valuable concession indeed to a theologian inclined to embarrassment. This insidious remark is a good instance of Fontenelle's antitheological tactics. But it is not in such feline strokes of the paw, that the bias of the book is most apparent. It is rather in the complete absence of any religious sentiment, or even poetical emotion at all. The author shows himself blankly unreceptive of the feelings which, a hundred years later, would stir the imagination of a Kant, when contemplating the starry heavens. The *Origine des Fables* and the *Histoire des Oracles* are masterpieces of quiet malice. He tells us in the *Origine des Fables* that the history of all nations, Greeks, Gauls, Romans, Americans and Chinese, begins with fables . . . 'all nations, that is, except the Chosen People, among whom a special attention of Providence has preserved the truth.' Here the very qualification which saves the orthodoxy of the statement is made to gently insinuate its own improbability. In the *Histoire des Oracles*, a work adapted from the Dutch of one Van Dale, he establishes that the Pagan oracles were not the work of demons, and did not cease at the death of Christ. The thesis seems innocent enough, but Fontenelle's treatment of it leaves the reader with the conviction that demons and oracles of every kind are more than suspicious: a conviction which he must be slow-witted indeed not to be inclined to apply to Rome as much as to Delphi. Yet nothing has been said that would formally justify such a conclusion. Certainly his attack on revelation lost nothing in acuteness for being disguised under the mantle of an exquisitely pudic orthodoxy that shrank from the contagion of superstition.

Fontenelle reaches his greatest height of paradoxical brilliancy in his well-known *Dialogues des Morts*, published in 1686. Of this book Voltaire wrote to Frederic in 1751, 'Le défaut de Fontenelle, c'est qu'il veut toujours avoir de l'esprit. C'est toujours lui qu'on voit, et jamais ses héros; il leur fait dire le contraire de ce qu'ils devraient dire, il soutient le pour et le contre, il ne veut que briller.' Was that, after all, so grave a fault, good Master? And does the criticism come well from the author of *Saül* and other historical *facéties*? However we may explain this unfavourable judgment, and there is more than one alternative to its being the expression of unbiassed opinion, it remains a fact that Voltaire himself never wrote anything wittier than these imaginary conversations. Their *verve* is inimitable, and never flags for a moment, there is not a dull line in all the forty. Fontenelle chooses the most delightfully incongruous companions for the discussion of every subject under the sun. Faustina proves to Brutus that her conduct to Marcus Aurelius was of a most disinterested description and was dictated by the very same motives which led Brutus to murder his friend. Erastitrates, a physician of antiquity, considerably damps the enthusiasm of Harvey, over the benefits which his discovery has conferred on mankind, by the remark that he does not observe any diminution in the number of annual arrivals on the shores of Styx. Socrates explains to Montaigne that antiquity was a poor affair after all, and that there were just as many fools and knaves in the Athens of his day, as in the Paris which Montaigne knew.

The *Dialogues* gives us the answer to the question of Fontenelle's scepticism. As we have seen, he was no sceptic in matters of religion, being definitely anti-religious on positive grounds; nor was he a sceptic in what he called experimental philosophy, *i.e.* science, where he found indeed his one point of certitude. Where he was a sceptic was in morals. Not that he doubted that the guidance of reason was what men required in order to be good and happy, but he more than suspected that the nature of things did not in fact permit such a result, except in so small a minority of cases as to leave the world, in the main, a stage for knaves and fools. The wise should be encouraged to get what amusement they could from the spectacle. He used to say in later years, that the amount of enthusiasm around him frightened him. The important thing to note about this temperamental attitude—for, although he may have supported it by argument, it was that *au fond*—is its difference from that of the second generation of the eighteenth century, of the philosophers who carried the movement of emancipation into the political sphere. One sees the sort of imaginary dialogue which Fontenelle would have put on the lips of, say, Turgot and Machiavelli.

His other important work is his *Mémoires* of the Academy of the Sciences, of which he was perpetual secretary. It was one of his duties to write *éloges* of the deceased academicians. For once Cydias becomes almost enthusiastic and really eloquent. He realised the dignity and beauty of these workers' lives, and he makes us feel them in a series of short biographies which really can hardly be too highly praised. The simple virtues of these great men, their probity, their immense and peaceful labours, their delightful piety, like that of Ozanan, who said it belonged to the Sorbonne to dispute, to the Pope to decide, and to the mathematician to go to Heaven in a perpendicular straight line; or their simplicity, like that of the great chemist who said of the Regent: 'Je le connais, j'ai fréquenté dans son laboratoire. Oh, c'est un rude travailleur!'—all the features of their blameless existences are lovingly and carefully detailed. We are surprised to find another Fontenelle, very different to the author of the *Dialogues des Morts*, a Fontenelle who does not sneer, who has almost forgotten to be epigrammatic. Almost, but not quite. We are told that M. Dodart 'accompagnait de toutes les lumières de la raison la respectable obscurité de la foi.' Science had seized him, and having seized him never let him go. His nimble brain moved easily in what he called experimental philosophy. And it is in his services to science—not the services of an independent discoverer, but the no less necessary ones of the writer who familiarises the world with the results obtained by specialists in their laboratory or at their telescope—that his real contribution to his time and the transitional movement of his time consists. He died happily and peacefully, aged ninety-nine years and eleven months, with the characteristic words on his lips: 'J'éprouve une difficulté d'être.' And the Académie des Sciences has never had such a good secretary since.

PROSPER MÉRIMÉE

THE centenary of Prosper Mérimée four years ago, passed practically unnoticed, which is perhaps what that eminent person, who had an almost comical horror of popular appreciation, would have liked. One can imagine the sort of letter he would have written on September 27, 1903, to some 'Unknown Friend' among the shades in description of the celebration of his memory, if, in fact, his compatriots had remembered him. As it is, they saved him the trouble. 'A few words' were murmured by that veteran Professor of the Sorbonne, M. Emile Faguet, an article appeared here and there in the French press, but these voices had little, if any, echo. Perhaps the official world of M. Combes was detached from such purely academic interests. The fact is that Mérimée, alive or dead, is not available for the objects of popular propaganda. Both as a man and as an artist his appeal was, and still is, to a small circle. It may be worth our while to try and discover in what the value of that appeal consists.

The extreme conscientiousness and integrity of soul of the artist renders it justifiable to seek that value not only in his written word. Mérimée's personality was a work of art as sincerely conceived, as deftly composed, as logically worked out as any of his own stories. So his personality may come, in fairness, to be considered as more than an essential element in—rather as one, and that an essential aspect of—his contribution, the 'moi haïssable' (so great an artist was he in life as well as letters), being as dexterously concealed in the daily habit of the man of the world, the *mondain*, as in the pages of the writer.

It would doubtless have annoyed him excessively to be told that the key to the success with which he handled such a multiplicity and complexity of interests, was to be found in the pages of the *Imitation of Christ*; yet few men have carried out so consistently the exhortation, 'Sibi unitus et simplificatus esse.' I shall therefore make no apology for adopting here a method of criticism which is, in most cases, rightly held to be illegitimate. Artistic creation is nearly always a special function of the brain, and, for the most part, unrelated, at least obviously, to the rest of the artist's life.

Prosper Mérimée was born a hundred years ago on September 28th. His father, Jean-François

Leonor, was a painter of mediocre quality who, after some moderate success with the brush, had intelligence enough to recognise his own calibre and to resign the practice of painting for its study. He became professor at the École Polytechnique and Secretary of the École des Beaux-Arts. He was the author of a history of oil painting, and spent much of his time in his laboratory experimenting on the chemical constituents of colours. Jean-François, when in middle life, met in a pension, where he gave lessons, a girl named Anna Moreau, neither rich nor beautiful, whom he married. The mother of Prosper would seem to have been a remarkable woman. M. Filon describes her as 'un caractère ferme, un esprit prompt, de nature sèche et gaie.' He adds that she was peacefully and invincibly irreligious, the reverse of sentimental, and very faithful to her duties and her affections. She painted with some skill, and was a fascinating *raconteuse.* Her portraits of children gained her a certain reputation, and are said to have owed part of their success to the way in which she fixed the attention of her young models by the delightful stories with which she would beguile the hours of sitting. In a word, she was just the mother indicated for Mérimée on Schopenhauer's theory of heredity. At least it would appear that Prosper inherited his brain from her;

and that not merely in the sense of intellectual power alone, but also in the whole turn and cast of his mind. In her we see his love of anecdote (his best work consists really of exquisitely finished anecdote), his horror of sentimentality, of *pleurnicherie*, his aversion to religion of all kinds.

In 1821 François Mérimée wrote to his friend Fabre, a painter of Montpellier, who had succeeded Alfieri in the affections of the Countess of Albany: 'J'ai un grand fils de dix-huit ans dont je voudrais bien faire un avocat . . . toujours *élevé* à la maison, il a de bonnes mœurs et de l'instruction.'

Reading for the Bar in Paris, as in London, is not incompatible with other and more romantic interests, and the future Academician found time to make many literary friends. J. J. Ampère and Albert Stapfer were among his intimates. Stapfer was an interesting and charming person, the son of the Swiss minister. He represented a type far too rare among us to-day, though frequently to be met with a hundred years ago, being indeed a survival from the eighteenth century. Endowed with considerable literary ability, he seems to have lacked personal ambition or the desire for money, and was content to remain a spectator of the battles of letters, excelling in intimacy as a wise critic and brilliant talker. Such men are the salt of society; in the eighteenth century they alone constituted the literary 'public.' Mérimée used to frequent the house of Stapfer's father, now retired from diplomacy and definitely settled in Paris in the midst of the intellectual society he loved.

Here the 'jeunes' used to assemble. While their elders counted their honours at whist, they would gather in a corner round a stout, dark, square-faced man with little flaming eyes. It was no less a personage than Stendhal. Sometimes his hearers were distracted by the fluent rhetoric of a young professor of philosophy, Victor Cousin, on which occasions the great man would grunt with impatience and growl forth the characteristic appreciation: 'Depuis Bossuet personne n'a joué de la blague sérieuse comme cet homme-là!'

And here we must dwell for a moment on the influence of Stendhal over Mérimée, who, fortunately, has left us an invaluable document on his one and only master. These few pages on Henri Beyle in his *Portraits Historiques et Littéraires*, tell us quite as much about their writer as their subject. Our criticisms of our friends not unfrequently represent the reactions they produce in ourselves, unconsciously objectified. Mérimée in the particular case has admitted as much to one of his unknown correspondents, though he has declared in his published study of Stendhal that, except for certain literary preferences and aversions, they had scarcely an idea in common. That this should have been so, at least at the moment of their first meeting in 1820, is not surprising, Beyle being then about forty, and Mérimée barely eighteen.

Beyle's formula is somewhat complex. A true disciple of the eighteenth century, of Diderot and the Encyclopædists, he was nevertheless the father of French nineteenth-century literature and the authentic founder of the Romantic movement. Victor Hugo did but invent the mediæval staging that gave that movement its vogue in the drawing-rooms of the Restoration, and it was the splendour of his genius that caused the play to become identified with the scenery in the public imagination. There was no necessary connection between the ideals of Christianity and the Romantic movement. Indeed the spirit of its founder was emphatically anti-Christian in the eighteenth-century manner of D'Alembert, Condorcet, and Voltaire. The movement was primarily a reaction against the conventions which had enslaved the French drama, and, so far, represented the claim of literature to find its value in a true observation and sincere rendering of human life. To be a 'Romantic' in 1824 meant that one despised the sacred 'Unities,' that one laughed at the Abbé Auger; that one had the temerity to find Racine conventional and unsatisfying. Beyle's pamphlet, *Racine and Shakespeare*, in which the latter poet's truthfulness of observation, and daring disregard of the axioms of a pedantic classicism are contrasted with the former's rhetorical representation of the life of the passions in a passionless vacuum of abstraction, was the manifesto of the first period of the Romantic movement, as the preface of Hugo's *Cromwell* was of the second.

A foolish person once asked Beyle his profession. 'Observateur du cœur humain,' replied the novelist; and it is said that the foolish person fled, convinced that the reply was a euphemism for police-spy. The phrase certainly stands not unfitly on the threshold of the nineteenth century, as the formula of nearly all that century's literary production. To it may be attached not only the works of the Romantics properly so-called, but the 'roman de mœurs,' the psychological novel, and the labours of the self-styled naturalists. In personal character Beyle seems to have been a puzzling mass of contradictions. He claimed to be always guided by 'la *Lo*gique' (as he emphasised the word in pronunciation), but never, according to Mérimée, was there a more impulsive and spontaneous creature. He imagined that he had discovered his ideal of passion (up to which he lived as well as wrote, in Italy). He had doubtless found there abundant materials for its incarnation, but the ideal is as old and universal as the 'Fall.' His views on this subject were, in fact, as elementary as they well could be in a civilised man, and his appreciation of women was precisely on a par with his criticism of religion. As to the latter, whatever they might say, the professors of all forms of religion were necessarily hypocrites. His curious belief in the absolute equality of the human mind precluded the charitable alternative—fools. The parallel may be left to complete itself. It is nevertheless fair to note that the experience which was to Beyle the crown of life 'Beyle croyait qu'il n'y avait de bonheur possible en ce monde que pour un homme amoureux,' writes Mérimée—was always to him psychological and emotional rather than purely physical; it was always love—of sorts—not vice. In all this he was a true child of the eighteenth century. That century dealt invariably in absolute judgments. Austere philosophers like d'Alembert and Condorcet would have endorsed Beyle's religious views, and would have had, at least, a theoretic sympathy with his attitude in sexual matters. As regards the criticism of religions, the glimmerings of a genuine historical method had not dawned on their consciousness, and the Christian theory of continence, which they regarded not altogether unjustifiably as in practice the supreme hypocrisy of the Church, was to them a very βδέλυγμα τῆς ἐρημώσεως of the human spirit.

It is easy to point out the insufficiency of the anti-religious dogmatism of the Encyclopædists. Here, however, we are not concerned with philosophy for its own sake, but only as a social element in reaction.

The cataclysm of the Revolution had buried the *ancien régime*, and with it, for a time at least, the lofty hopes which had animated many of the thinkers who had unconsciously done most to render possible that time of terror. The Napoleonic epic intoxicated the opening years of the new century with a chalice of blood and glory: Europe awoke sceptical and weary after the double nightmare. And France, who had given this terrible object-lesson to the rest of the world, was no less disillusioned. Now Mérimée was a prince of 'désillusionnés.'

Sainte-Beuve heard from the lips of Madame Mérimée an anecdote of Prosper's childhood which seemed to him to give the key to his character. He committed some childish fault at the age of five, which induced his mother to place him *en pénitence* outside the door of the studio where she was working. Through the door the child implored her pardon, making the most convincing protestations of contrition. His mother paid no attention. At last he opened the door, and dragged himself towards her on his knees in so grotesquely pathetic an attitude that she could not prevent herself bursting into laughter. He changed his tone, and said, rising: 'Eh bien, puisqu'on se moque de moi, je ne demanderai jamais plus pardon!' He kept, says Sainte-Beuve, his resolution only too well. And his fidelity to it was the true source of his profound irony. Years afterwards Sainte-Beuve added to his note of the anecdote a last reflection: 'S'il avait su le Grec à cet âge, il aurait pu prendre la devise qu'il porta gravée sur un cachet: Μέμνησ' ἀπιστεῖν, Souviens-toi de méfier.'

We may accept the story for what it may be worth, not forgetting that distrust of men and things was in the psychological climate into which Mérimée was born. Kant seemed to have clipped for ever the wings of philosophy; post-Kantian idealism had not yet attained its *droit de cité* in the commonwealth of European thought, and if it had, it may be doubted whether so cautious and cool a head as Mérimée's would have yielded to its seductions. The apparently appalling results of popular enthusiasm in the holiest of all causes—the cause of them that sit in darkness, and in the shadow of death—had not been such as to encourage confidence in the immanent forces at work in the human process. The old comely universe over which, with benedictory episcopal hands, the 'Pater de cœlis Deus' of Christian tradition had presided, on the whole benignly, was swept away, and the promise of the new Heaven and Earth was but a faltering one at best. In that old world where, in spite of superficial disruptions, such as Black Deaths and Thirty Years' Wars, all was really secure, steadied by the Arms of the Eternal, it had been possible, it had come to many naturally, to live gracious and dignified lives of unremitting toil, serenely confident in a providential disposition of the fruits of their labours.

The 'fruits of philosophy' had just recently been bitter in the mouths of Frenchmen of that day. Reaction or disillusion seemed the only alternatives that lay before them. As a matter of fact Mérimée resigned himself to both. The stifling of French liberties by Louis Napoleon's *coup d'État* awoke no protest from him, and he became a Senator of that prince's short-lived Empire and Inspector of National Monuments, while his art, as we shall now proceed to see, was based on profound disillusion. Disillusion is a term which depends for its value on its context; it may mean gain or loss; what was the balance in the case of Mérimée?

He was born into a society but recently emancipated from the most effective and complete system of religious idealisation that the world has ever seen. There was no part of life to which that system did not extend, no human emotion which it had not made its own—for good or for ill. Not only by its own supreme emotional quality had it seized and retained the emotions, but by means of its transcendental values it had enormously increased their momentum in certain directions. The three fundamental theological virtues had dilated the psychological capacity of man to an extent that would have seemed impossible to a pre-Christian thinker. Infinite Truth as the possession of Faith, infinite bliss as the object of Hope, infinite love as the reward of Charity—such and no less formed the inalienable birthright of every member of the Catholic Church. We are not concerned here with theology or philosophy, and we may therefore note without further comment that, as a matter of fact, whatever its explanation, the prestige of that august conception of human destiny had become, in the opening years of the nineteenth century, very dim. Voltaire was not a final solvent of the claims of ecclesiastical authority, but, for the moment, he was an exceedingly effective one. Disillusion necessarily ensued, and it reached a depth of which the height of Christian aspiration furnished the measure.

It is true that Mérimée did not himself suffer the personal disillusion of the loss of belief. But generations of Christian heredity were behind him, and there is no doubt that the close reserve and impassivity of manner that made him resemble 'un Anglais, sauf le sourire,' says Taine, were the mask of a profoundly sensitive and emotional nature. His voluminous correspondence with his 'amies' reveals, as we shall see, an affectionate and tender temperament at which he himself was the first to mock.

Born into that clear dry air of rationalism, in which propositions crackle defiantly like pistol shots, his nature lacked the environment necessary for emotional expansion. So his view of life came to be based on a mistrust of emotional values, and also, it must be added, of those intellectual generalisations which many of them seem to imply. It must further be noted that Mérimée did not replace any of the lost illusions. He was not of those who believe the more ardently in humanity when they have lost their faith in God, who find their ideal on earth when Heaven has melted away. No; he lived contentedly, stoically at least, on the fine edge of complete disillusion:—

Veut-on savoir sa conception de la vie? Il l'enfermait dans une farce profonde qu'il a répétée plusieurs fois dans ses lettres. 'Arlequin tombait du cinquième étage.

Comme il passait à la hauteur du troisième, on lui demanda comment il se trouvait.' 'Très-bien, pourvu que cela dure.' La vie est une chute. D'où tombons-nous et où tombons-nous? On ne sait. Dans une seconde nous aurons les reins cassés, mais on est si bien en l'air!

Complete detachment from any dogmatic belief—nay, the passionate rejection of any such mental bonds—has not infrequently been allied with a highly sensitive religious temperament. Amiel is a case in point; he is, in fact, the prototype of such souls. Mérimée was, it must be owned, openly irreligious—'impie,' as the French say. Beyle, who delighted in being called the 'personal enemy of Providence,' had cultivated with complete success the elements of irreligion which his disciple had learnt, in the first instance, at his mother's knee. His philosophy was the pure materialism of Holbach and Helvetius; there were no half-tones, the setting sun had left no twilight behind. As the years and he grew grey together, he came, in a measure, to modify his attitude, although the fact that he did so was unknown, save to one, until the year 1897, when *Une Correspondance Inédite* was published in the *Revue des Deux Mondes*.

His correspondent in this series of letters was a deeply religious woman, and Mérimée was much attached to her. Her friendship brought out a side of his nature, little suspected by the librarian

Panizzi and Mlle. Jenny Dacquin, the recipient of the first *Lettres à une Inconnue.* In these pages we have a Mérimée who has made a careful study of the Gospels, who regrets his conscientious inability to accept Christianity, who can reach the point of saying: 'Dieu me semble très probable, et le commencement de l'Évangile de Saint Jean n'a rien qui me répugne.' But, so far as we know, except for the clause in his will directing prayers to be said at his grave by a Protestant minister, which looks suspiciously like a last stroke aimed at the religion of his country, or may have been perhaps a courteous concession to the feelings of the two devoted English ladies who nursed him on his deathbed, these *velléités* of belief never reached the consistency of a permanent mood or translated themselves into action.

Mérimée's literary contribution at first sight seems rather the product of the leisure of an accomplished man of the world than that of a professional man of letters. An accomplished man of the world he certainly was, wearing his immense learning with unobtrusive grace, willing to devote his time and erudition to making a success of country-house theatricals, devoted to little girls and cats, between which branches of the animal kingdom he maintained the existence of a mysterious affinity, a delightful companion, attractive as it would seem by a singular dispensation, to men and women and children alike—he was all this, but he was more also. He possessed a very special and individual view of art, which he was fortunate enough to be able to express almost perfectly. Indeed, his style, given his self-imposed limitations, is practically perfect, the only possible criticism on it being that the routine of its bland impeccability gives at times the suggestion of something inhuman. Never to make mistakes is surely to be more or less than man. And, in truth, his view of life of which his style is so perfect an equivalent—here, if ever, *le style c'est l'homme*—was not that of one who is himself involved in its delicious and absurd complications, its foolish tragedies, its comedies of tears. In his writings, if not in his life, he stands permanently aloof from the passions which he paints so perfectly. Never for an instant is he betrayed into partisanship for any of his puppets. José Lizarrabengoa and the Spanish gipsy, Arsène Guillot and Mme. de Piennes, Julie de Chavarny, Saint-Clair, the Abbé Aubain, Colomba, Don Juan de Marana, types terrible, pathetic, humorous, flit across his purified vision, which remains intent only on noting the beauty of their ever-changing combinations as they pass. His attitude is that of the eternal spectator, of the God whom Mephistopheles revealed to Doctor Faustus. That deity was no doubt immoral, and, from the human point of view which judges deities, so far, unsatisfactory. But to be an immoral God is the achievement of the artist.

Flaubert has left behind him his ideal of perfect anonymity, of the entire self-suppression of the writer in his creation. It was just this that Mérimée attained so supremely.

Take, for instance, the following passage from that flawless piece of work, *Carmen*:—

> Elle avait un jupon rouge fort court qui laissait voir des bas de soie blancs avec plus d'un trou, et des souliers mignons de maroquin rouge attachés avec des rubans couleur de feu. Elle écartait sa mantille afin de montrer ses épaules et un gros bouquet de cassie qui sortait de sa chemise. Elle avait encore une fleur de cassie dans le coin de la bouche, et elle s'avançait en se balançant sur ses hanches comme une pouliche du haras de Cordoue. Dans mon pays une femme en ce costume aurait obligé le monde à se signer. À Séville chacun lui adressait quelque compliment gaillard sur sa tournure; elle répondait à chacun, faisant des yeux en coulisse, le poing sur la hanche, effrontée comme une vraie bohémienne qu'elle était. D'abord elle ne me plut pas, et je repris mon ouvrage; mais elle, suivant l'usage des femmes et des chats qui ne viennent pas quand on les appelle et qui viennent quand ôn ne les appelle pas, s'arrêta devant moi et m'adressa la parole: 'Compère,' me dit-elle, à la façon andalouse, 'veux-tu me donner ta chaine pour tenir les clefs de mon coffre-fort?'—'C'est pour attacher mon épinglette,' lui repondis-je.—'Ton épinglette!' s'écria-t-elle en riant. 'Ah, Monsieur fait de la dentelle, puisqu'il a besoin

d'épingles!' Tout le monde qui était là se mit à rire, et moi je me sentais rougir, et je ne pouvais trouver rien à lui répondre. 'Allons, mon cœur,' reprit-elle, 'fais-moi sept aunes de dentelle noire pour une mantille, épinglier de mon âme!' et, prenant la fleur de cassie qu'elle avait à la bouche, elle me la lança, d'un mouvement de pouce, juste entre les deux yeux. Monsieur, cela me fit l'effet d'une balle qui m'arrivait. . . . Je ne savais où me fourrer, je demeurais immobile comme une planche. Quand elle fut entrée dans la manufacture, je vis la fleur de cassie qui était tombée à terre entre mes pieds; je ne sais ce qui me prit, mais je la ramassai sans que mes camarades s'en aperçussent et je la mis précieusement dans ma veste. Première sottise!

What splendid objectivity of treatment is here! How grandly the scene moves towards its conclusion—the treasuring of the flower from Carmen's wilful red mouth—and how deftly that conclusion sums up, in a gesture of self-committal, the process in the speaker's mind, never described, but thus inevitably revealed.

Such revelation of character compressed into a trait, fixed in a passing gesture, struck, as it were, once for all, in the clear outline of an antique medal, is the secret of his power of narrative. The daily actions of human beings are in great measure distressingly irrelevant; three parts of what we say and do does not really belong to us—it is more external to us than our clothes, being but the half-conscious reproduction in the mirror of the mind of what we see and hear around us. To discern amid this baffling whirl of quasi-automatic reaction the really significant 'Word,' the authentic movement of the conscious soul with all its most distant, most secret implications, and so to express all this that it reveal itself clearly, finally, with that inevitability of phrase which is the only hall-mark of true literary expression, is to be a great artist. Mérimée's reputation might well rest on this scene of the meeting of Don José and Carmen.

Nothing is further from his mind than any general philosophy of life. 'La métaphysique me plaît,' he writes to a correspondent, 'parceque cela ne finit jamais.' He is content with the concrete episode and confines himself to tracing the psychological connections of moods. In this way, however, he becomes a philosopher, *malgré lui*. Into the hundred pages of *Carmen* has gone the whole of Schopenhauer's metaphysic of Love and Death. *Arsène Guillot* is worth many learned treatises on popular religion and the psychology of the courtesan. Very significant too is his choice of subject. He seems not to have been much interested in those refinements and complications which increasing civilisation has worked into the woof of our passions. In this respect he and Mr. Henry James are at the antipodes of art. His characters are all quite simple, or at least their complexity does not go beyond the barely-veiled cunning of the savage. They are so dominated by the passion that leads them up to the dramatic issue of the story as to appear at times to be but embodiments of it. Not that they ever become mere abstract types. They are filled in with a wealth of detail, of plausible circumstantiality which makes them breathe full-blooded before us. Their hands grow hot or cold in ours, as we meet them at some tragic parting of their ways.

But everywhere and always they are puppets at the mercy of fate, and the cords with which their destiny at last strangles them, are twined out of their own passionate, wilful hearts. Life is a force—a '*Force Ennemie*'—which sweeps them on to the inevitable doom of human consciousness in such conditions.

The tragic simplicity of his characters is matched by the simplicity of the issues with which he prefers to deal. Just as they are among the least introspective of the great creations of fiction, so these issues are of the plainest and most direct. Love, jealousy, revenge, unchecked by philosophy or religion, form the staple of his matter. There is hardly one of his tales that does not involve more than one violent death. Appropriately he chooses his *mise-en-scène* among Andalusian gipsies, or in the brigand-infested *maquis* of Corsica, or in wild

Lithuanian forests, where sorceresses dwell. The naïve immorality of his personages finds thus a congruous setting. For, in truth, Mérimée paints pre-moral man before he had fully emerged from the womb of his great Mother 'red in tooth and claw.'

Of the subsequent process by which, in patient length of centuries, reason developed with its derivatives, religion and civilisation, of the slow, gradual formation of other than purely egotistic values, he has little, if anything, to say: these things do not interest him, they do not possess the dramatic quality which he seeks. Of the world of inner tragedy of a Hamlet or a St. Augustine he knows nothing.

One of his most powerful stories, *Colomba*, possesses in a high degree this sombre beauty of a humanity that we still feel stirring in the recesses of our inherited being.

Colomba is a Corsican maiden who is a living incarnation of the dominant passion of her island race. The one duty of Corsicans is revenge. They do not seem to have reached, at the beginning of the nineteenth century, that stage of civil development known as the law for composition of blood. So strict is their devotion to duty that one wonders how their bloodthirsty stock has survived. They have come to take a disinterested pleasure in the performance of these sinister actions for their own sake in virtue of a well-known law of social development. One Pietri dies an exceptional and natural death. His son exclaims at his father's funeral: 'Oh, pourquoi n'es-tu pas mort de la *malemort* (mala morte)? Nous t'aurions vengé!' And one feels his regret to be excusable, indeed inevitable.

Colomba's father has been treacherously murdered about a year before the opening of the story. She suspects the hand of a rival family, the Barracini, who are, however, able to exculpate themselves legally. One may imagine how much value that has in Colomba's eyes. So she sets to work aided by two friendly brigands, who live concealed—*latitanti*, as Italians still say of their descendants to-day—in the jungle or *maquis* that covers more than half the island, to weave the web of evidence. She discovers a forgery here, there an altered date in the documents on which the Barracini relied to prove their innocence. Her case complete, she hands over the sacred charge to her brother, an officer in the French army. Ors' Anton, however, has imbibed the prejudices of civilisation during a prolonged residence on the Continent. He doubts his sister's evidence, and, in any case, would be for legal proceedings. A degenerate indeed!

A un demi-mille du village, après bien des détours,

Colomba s'arrêta tout-à-coup dans un endroit où le chemin faisait un coude. Là s'élevait une petite pyramide de branchages, les uns verts, les autres desséchés, amoncelés à la hauteur de trois pieds environ. Du sommet on voyait percer l'extrémité d'une croix de bois peinte en noir. Dans plusieurs cantons de la Corse, surtout dans les montagnes, un usage extrêmement ancien, et qui se rattache peut-être à des superstitions du paganisme, oblige les passants à jeter une pierre ou un rameau d'arbre, sur le lieu ou un homme a péri de mort violente. Pendant de longues années, aussi longtemps que le souvenir de sa fin tragique demeure dans la mémoire des hommes, cette offrande singulière s'accumule de jour en jour. On appelle cela l'amas, le *mucchio* d'un tel. Colomba s'arrêta devant ce tas de feuillage, et arrachant une branche d'arbousier l'ajouta à la pyramide.

'Orso,' dit-elle, 'c'est ici que notre père est mort. Prions pour son âme, mon frère!' et elle se mit à genoux. Orso l'imita aussitôt. En ce moment la cloche du village tinta lentement, car un homme était mort dans la nuit. Orso fondit en larmes.

Au bout de quelques minutes Colomba se leva, l'œil sec, mais la figure animée. Elle fit du pouce à la hâte le signe de croix familier à ses compatriotes et qui accompagne d'ordinaire leurs serments solennels; puis, entraînant son frère, elle reprit le chemin du village. Ils rentrèrent en silence dans leur maison. Orso monta dans sa chambre. Un instant après Colomba l'y suivit, portant une petite cassette qu'elle posa sur la table. Elle l'ouvrit et en tira une chemise couverte de larges taches de sang.

'Voici la chemise de votre père, Orso,' et elle le jeta sur ses genoux.

'Voici le plomb qui l'a frappé,' et elle posa sur la chemise deux balles oxydées.

'Orso, mon frère!' cria-t-elle en se précipitant dans ses

bras et l'étreignant avec force, 'Orso! tu le vengeras!' et elle l'embrassa avec une espèce de fureur, baisa les balles et la chemise, et sortit de la chambre, laissant son frère comme pétrifié sur sa chaise.

Colomba's designs are at last crowned with success. After a meeting, for purposes of reconciliation, with the Barracini (insisted on by the préfet), at which they are convicted of perjury and corruption on the evidence of a bandit, called M. le Curé, the two sons of the Barracini lie in wait for Orso and attempt to assassinate him. He kills them both in self-defence. The twelve-year-old niece of the bandit, Chilina, carries the news to Colomba and satisfies her of her brother's safety.

'Les autres!' demanda Colomba d'une voix rauque. Chillina fit le signe de la croix avec l'index et le doigt du milieu. Aussitôt une vive rougeur succéda, sur la figure de Colomba, à sa pâleur mortelle. Elle jeta un regard ardent sur la maison des Barracini, et dit en souriant à ses hôtes: 'Rentrons prendre le café.'

That 'Rentrons prendre le café' is magnificent!

The description of the procession bringing home to their father, the bodies of the young Barracini is like a piece of an antique frieze.

Le jour était déjà fort avancé lorsqu'une triste procession entra dans le village. On rapportait à l'avocat Barracini les cadavres de ses enfants, chacun couché en travers d'une mule que conduisait un paysan. Unc foulc de clients et d'oisifs suivait le lugubre cortège. Avec eux on voyait les gendarmes qui arrivent toujours trop tard, et l'adjoint, qui levait les bras au ciel, répétant sans cesse: 'Que dira M. le préfet?' Quelques femmes, entre autres une nourrice d'Orlanduccio, s'arrachaient les cheveux et poussaient des hurlements sauvages. Mais leur douleur bruyante produisait moins d'impression que le désespoir muet d'un personnage qui attirait tous les regards. C'était le malheureux père, qui allait d'un cadavre à l'autre, soulevait leurs têtes, souillées de terre, baisait leurs lèvres violettes, soutenait leurs membres déjà roidis, comme pour leur éviter les cahots de la route. Parfois on le voyait ouvrir la bouche pour parler, mais il n'en sortait pas un cri, pas une parole. Toujours les yeux fixés sur les cadavres, il se heurtait contre les pierres, contre les arbres, contre tous les obstacles qu'il rencontrait.

And with this we will take leave of Colomba, among the most sombre and tragic of Mérimée's creations. In constructing this type of primitive humanity, at once so terrifying and so beautiful, he returned to the primal sources of Art, for *Primus in orbe deos fecit timor.*

Mérimée was more than a writer of stories, though it is undoubtedly by them that he will live. He composed several volumes of history, published some admirable archæological studies—the fruits of his labours as Inspector of National Monuments —and wrote several plays. He 'commenced author' as a dramatist with his *Cromwell,* which Stendhal praised highly. He followed this up with his imaginary *Théâtre de Clara Gazul.* This volume contained several short dramas, of which the two best are *Les Espagnols en Danemark* and *Le Ciel et L'Enfer*, professing on the title-page to be a translation of the work of one Clara Gazul, 'la célèbre comédienne espagnole.' Such literary tricks were much in fashion in those days. Probably no one was deceived, more particularly as the frontispiece displayed, as the portrait of the supposed authoress, a caricature of Mérimée himself in a low dress by his friend Etienne Delecluze. Nevertheless, the cleverness of the *postiche* was such that a Spaniard was reported to have said: 'Yes, the translation is not bad; but what would you say if you knew the original?' He used his talent for mystification still more cleverly in the *La Guzla*, which was given to the world as a collection of Dalmatian ballads. He has told us the circumstances in a preface written in 1840. Local colour was the Holy Grail of the young Romantics. But how paint local colour without travel, and how travel without money? Mérimée quotes the recipe which he gave to his friend J.-J. Ampère:

> Racontons notre voyage, imprimons-en le récit, et avec la somme que cette publication nous rapportera nous irons voir si le pays ressemble à nos déscriptions.

Mérimée invented a bard of the name of Maglanovich, whose ballads he professed to translate.

He added numerous pseudo-philological notes, a pedantic dissertation on Vampires and the Evil Eye, and a plausible biography of the bard. This time the success was complete. Pouchkine, the Russian poet, was completely taken in, and translated several pieces as curious specimens of the Illyrian genius. Mérimée sums up the episode in a very characteristic conclusion: 'à partir de ce jour je fus dégoûté de la couleur locale, en voyant combien il est aisé de la fabriquer.' When local colour fails, what remains for the sceptical Romantic?

We have seen how Mérimée's scepticism affected his art, influencing him in his choice of subject, driving him back from the problems of civilisation to the more spontaneous interplay of passion and impulse in a less sophisticated humanity, driving him outward from the study of the soul to the observation of fact. That collective process of reason which we call civilisation was a snare useful for impressing the bourgeois; equally the individual process which we call a human character was without intrinsic interest, and derived its value for art from the casual combinations into which it might enter with others on the stage of time. And in all this he was a disciple of Stendhal. But he was a disciple with a difference.

Stendhal, in spite of his genius, could never tell

a story, and his style—he never revised—was both clumsy and careless. Mérimée could not write a really bad sentence, and was one of the best *raconteurs* that ever lived. To the philosophy of Stendhal, which remained substantially his own, he brought a much more strictly disciplined intelligence, and, in spite of his deliberate cynicism, a high degree of that indefinable quality called nobility of heart. The lives of the two men, as well as their literary productions, afford evidence of this. The ideas of Stendhal, for instance, in the matter of love were so well known that the authorship of Casanova's *Memoirs* was for a short time plausibly attributed to him, and it may fairly be doubted whether he would have been in the least inclined to resist the impeachment of having been the hero of any of the adventures of that egregious Venetian. Mérimée was also all his life an *homme à femmes*, but he was of too fine a make to find satisfaction in the embraces of the Venus of the *coulisse* or the *carrefour*. He was no saint, as the phrase is; but he knew that there are at least fifty thousand ways of enjoying the society of women, and he was capable of pity and self-control.

J'allais être amoureux (he writes to an unknown correspondent) quand je suis parti pour l'Espagne. La personne qui a causé mon voyage n'en a jamais rien su. Si j'étais resté, j'aurais peut-être fait une grande sottise, celle d'offrir à une femme digne de tout le bonheur dont on peut jouir sur la terre, de lui offrir dis-je, en échange de la perte de toutes ces choses qui lui étaient chères, une tendresse que je sentais moi-même très inférieure au sacrifice qu'elle aurait peut-être fait.

Not all those who proclaim loudly a more romantic view of the matter would be capable of such generous delicacy.

The more intimate side of Mérimée's nature, studiously concealed in his fiction, appears clearly enough in his correspondence. It is a fascinating compound of tenderness and mistrust, of sensitive pride at times overthrown by an irresistible need of emotional expansion and the spontaneous abandonment of a deeply affectionate nature. Much of his sentimental life is rightly buried for ever. The devotional scruples of his mistress brusquely cut short his first *liaison*. His second lasted eighteen years—the average length of a French government, says M. Filon. This too came to an end, not on account of scruples, but because the beloved grew cold. Mérimée suffered horribly. 'Mes souvenirs même ne me restent plus,' he writes to a friend. He puzzles his head over the reasons for his mistress's change. 'Un remords peut-être, mais je suis presque sûr qu'il n'y a pas de prêtre dans l'affaire.' Ah! his enemy was Time, the one eternal priest who, sooner or later, washes away our loves and hates, our sins and our virtues alike. He himself had not been in this affair quite beyond reproach. The correspondence with Mlle. Jenny Dacquin must have been carried on, at least in part, coincidently. This voluminous sheaf of letters, published in 1874 under the title *Lettres à une Inconnue*, reveals in Mérimée a somewhat *exigeant* but truly devoted lover, and, in his correspondent, a singularly tiresome mistress. Their characters were too much alike for them to be happy. She was too much of a Mérimée *en femme*. Both had the same fear of the open sea, and preferred hugging the shores of their respective egotisms; and his shore was lined with bristling rocks and dangerous shoals.

'Le bonheur lui manquait,' says Taine. If happiness failed him, it was not for lack of those external conditions which are usually held sufficient to produce it. He was rich, popular, successful; but happiness is a subjective quality, and there was that in his nature which made him his own worst enemy. He could never let himself go. He was always more afraid of error than anxious for truth. This constant fear of deception led him perhaps into the greatest of all. For, in life, he was by no means all that he might have been, and, in Art, his place, though certainly of the highest, is narrow.

FERDINAND FABRE

When Gibbon delicately pointed his remarks on the 'immorality' of the clergy during the dark ages, with the reflection that it was, after all, the virtues rather than the vices of that body which were dangerous to society, he went far to redeem himself, by anticipation, from the charge of superficiality fastened on him by the great ecclesiastical advocate of our day.

At least, he thereby indicated his opinion that so vast a topic as the social effects of Christianity could not be fruitfully discussed on such a side-issue as the moral defects which priests may happen to share with their untonsured brethren. And although this may appear to-day a very obvious commonplace, it represented in the eighteenth century—the century of Condorcet and Voltaire—a degree of philosophic calm on the subject which too many philosophers failed to reach. 'Les philosophes du 18ème siècle, trop disposés à croire que l'homme est toujours et partout le même, se figuraient volontiers les apôtres comme des capucins fripons.' Yes, but apostles are not always and everywhere rogues, and the implication hardly became the men who were so anxious, in their turn, to try their hands at the regeneration of society. It is to be feared that even now, in our cultured midst, prepossessions of the same nature as those which dominated these powerful but one-sided thinkers are not altogether dead. They still flourish, for instance, in what Viscount Morley once amiably called the dregs of the ecclesiastical world, and, for that matter, of the anti-ecclesiastical world also. Nay, even for those who aim at the not so common virtue of intellectual integrity, it is by no means easy in the particular case to be sure of objective vision, of 'seeing the object as it really is,' for, it is hardly possible that our view of the social effects of Christianity should be unaffected by our view of Christianity itself. And that attitude is so largely determined, as one of the greatest and saddest of human geniuses has told us, by reasons of the heart of which the reason knows nothing.

Attempts in the direction of such inquiry have frequently been made, both by the defenders and the opponents of Christianity. And in this circumstance, perhaps, lies the secret of their inconclusiveness. For the offices of judge and advocate cannot be confused without detriment to the verdict. Reference has already been made to the bigotry prevailing among the French anti-Christian thinkers of the eighteenth century. They did but take their cue from the defenders of orthodoxy. In England too, such hostile critics as Collins and Tindal were hardly more acrimonious and foul-mouthed, than a Christian bishop like Warburton.

Like modern scientific psychology, which has devoted itself to carrying out the programme indicated by Taine in the memorable words: 'C'est à l'âme que le science va se prendre,' the nineteenth-century novel occupied itself with a close scrutiny of the soul of man, so close indeed as sometimes to forget its artistic purpose, relapsing now and again into the pure science which was the backbone of its method. A literature based on Taine's programme, and guided by an insatiable curiosity to seek the precise measure of every ascertainable aspect of the contemporary soul, could not fail, sooner or later, to find itself confronted by religion.

The way in which man worships the gods is surely at least as important as the way in which he loves; and we know, to satiety, the value attributed by modern masters of the novel to the latter propensity. Apart, moreover, from the psychology of the individual, religion in its public aspect is a form of social life, and, in that capacity also, challenges the criticism of the modern novelist. Thus it seems to have come about that, under the influence of a spirit essentially non-religious and non-metaphysical, a spirit, that is, which, by hypothesis, abstains from absolute conclusions as much as from preconceived ideas, a possible method has been found for a fruitful criticism of the religious phenomenon. We cannot derive any precise information about religion in mid-Victorian England or the France of the Second Empire from the most careful study of the Book of Common Prayer or the Catechism of the Council of Trent, but 'le petit fait bien choisi,' Trollope's vignettes of the Barsetshire clergy, or Fabre's studies of ecclesiastical life in contemporary France, can tell us a great deal on the subject. The indirect method of such criticism is also largely in favour of its results, for it reduces to a minimum, what may be called the friction of the critic's personality.

'Had I written an epic about clergymen,' says Trollope, 'I would have taken St. Paul for my model; but, describing, as I have endeavoured to do, such clergymen as I see around me, I could not venture to be transcendental.' That is to say that Trollope writes of the clergy as they happen to occur in the society in which he finds them; they are described from outside as social phenomena, not from within as spiritual forces. It were impossible to consider the matter from a sounder point of view for the purpose in hand.

Now the Church of England in Trollope's day showed to great advantage by this method of portraiture. Many of the country clergy were men of good family, not a few of them reaching a far higher standard of education than was common at that time among the English upper class. They were also generally men of high moral character; in short they fulfilled admirably, on the whole, the purposes for which an established Church may be supposed to exist in the idea of a broad-minded statesman. The village spires of England pointed to an ideal in harmony with the best actual elements of the nation's life.

The Church may have been, in Lord Beaconsfield's phrase, still reeling from the effects of Newman's secession, but the shock had not made itself felt much in the country cathedral chapters, nor had the backwash of the Tractarian movement as yet settled itself into the current of modern Anglo-Catholicism. The Anglicanism of Barchester stood serene and strong in the consciousness of possession, not only of the spiritual values demanded and appreciated by the consciences of the faithful, but of those earthly values also, which, in their secular accumulations, had fairly come to represent, as in fact they had originally expressed, the appreciation of the faithful.

The Church of England stood in those days, for a fact; was indeed itself a great representative fact,—to wit, the people of England from a religious standpoint. To those old-fashioned divines, whose blameless lives Trollope paints so delightfully, religion was no matter of idea at all, it stood or fell as a fact, compact indeed of venerable precedent and present dignity of circumstance, but still as solid and undeniable as the fabric of the cathedral in which they preached. As such they preached it, and as such their hearers accepted or declined it. This may not have been a transcendental attitude, but there was philosophy in it too.

Take the scene of the bishop's death in the opening chapter of *Barchester Towers* which is one of truly fine comedy, in Mr. Meredith's sense of the word. It is also an English, an Anglican scene. Nowhere else on the face of the earth could such a scene have occurred just like that. Archdeacon Grantley 'certainly did desire to play first fiddle; he did desire to sit in full lawn sleeves among the peers of the realm,' and he did desire, if the truth must be out, to be called 'My Lord' by his reverend brethren. Innocent ambitions after all! And ambitions not differing in kind from those of all professional men, as Trollope in the same chapter remarks. Very different was the ambition of Hildebrand. Here we may observe an authentic note of the Church of England of that day. The psychological characteristics, the faults and virtues of the clergy were those belonging not essentially to a priesthood but rather to all men indifferently. The moral eminence on which the clergyman stood—his ordination vows and Sunday preaching—made a background against which those characteristics were more clearly visible than in the case of most men, but the qualities themselves were common to all. The fact is that the Christianity of Barchester Close, in spite of its goodly array of dean, prebendaries, minor canons and vicars-choral, was, in accordance with the national temper of mind, emphatically non-sacerdotal.

The picture of the Church of England in Trollope's pages represents that institution as reflecting the best elements of the nation's life, its wholesome morality, its respect for law and order, its love of justice combined with a singular inability to recognise a concrete case of injustice when sanctified by tradition. It must be admitted also that certain other elements are not wanting. An heroic impenetrability to ideas, a loathing of change, a pride of place and circumstance that is not always according to reason. But, on the whole, it is a great picture of a noble spiritual fabric which like our 'glorious constitution,' of which it is a part, a special aspect, points to no individual founder, stands for no special idea, but has come to be what it is through its own spontaneous development as representative of the nation's spiritual attitude, modified by, and in turn reacting on, the secular elements of the nation's growth.

It is a far cry from the gray, peaceful, rook-haunted towers of Barchester to the French cathedral town of Lormières; as far as from the methods and the point of view of Anthony Trollope to those of Ferdinand Fabre. This powerful writer, though little known in England, was one of the most important minor novelists of the Second Empire. Indeed, one can only call him minor in reference to his narrow range of subject—(he specialised in priests)—and his relatively small output. Sainte-Beuve praised his work in the highest terms. He just missed his *fauteuil* through the theological animosities created by his novels. Some of the Immortals voted against him because his writings were anti-religious, and some because they were too clerical. Pasteur was among his opponents on the former ground. His personal views (if he had any) were never revealed by him to any one. There is a tale of an indiscreet journalist who, in the course of interviewing his widow, asked her point-blank what her husband's religious beliefs had been. He could get no answer but a silent smile. His youth at least was religious. Like Renan, he was a seminarist who discovered before it was too late that he had no vocation. And he certainly retained from his training, as did Renan, a good deal of the priest. He handles problems of conduct with professional delicacy of touch, with a true moral sympathy, and yet, from the point of view of one who himself stands outside the web of sorrow and passion in which weaker ones are entangled. You feel that he touches such cases tenderly, compassionately, like a physician of the soul. His sympathy also for those of his characters in whom the ecclesiastical type of virtue is fully developed, is clear enough. Not that this sympathy ever blurs his vision. In *Les Courbezons*, one of his most admirably executed characters, a miracle of Christian charity and pure-hearted devotion, creates misery all around him through his inability to practise such elementary virtues as foresight and thrift. The man's admiration for the qualities he describes so well does not prevent the artist seeing through and beyond them.

It was partly his inability to interest himself in the personages of the modern novel, combined with the accidental circumstance of his ecclesiastical training, that led Fabre to his chosen subject.

'Assurément ces personnages, — le mari, la femme et l'amant,—qui défraient le roman contemporain, qui le défraieront peut-être toujours, car les combinaisons entre ces trois facteurs sont impérissables comme la vie elle-même, offraient un intérêt tres vif. Mais comment arrivait-il que ces combinaisons, tantôt ingénieuses, tantôt puissantes, me laissaient froid? . . . Dans l'Eglise au contraire j'étais saisi, touché tout de suite. Il n'était pas un détail du bénitier au tabernacle, dans la domaine des choses, du plus humble desservant au souverain pontife, dans la domaine des hommes, qui empreint pour moi de quelque souvenir suave ou terrible, ne me remuât tête et cœur.' From the point of view of modern literature the Church means the Priest; on the priest then Fabre concentrated his powers of observation and description.

That mysterious figure, the foster-father of civilisation and, in turn, its bitterest enemy, is indeed of a nature to interest the psychological inquirer. A man and yet not a man, for he is both more and less than a man, the Catholic priest is the true descendant of all the medicine-men and soothsayers of the past, as he is the most complete and finished expression of the idea which they all more or less successfully incarnated. That idea briefly comes to this: that the unknown force of the universe, the source of life from which we come and to which after our brief wandering we must return, being animated by an intelligence and will akin to the human, can be approached by us in our own interests, *more humano*. A priesthood exists in order to regulate and assure the success of our commerce with the Divine Unknown.

Some God or specially inspired prophet has established the conditions of the compact between men and the Divine, and priests are the appointed channel by which the graces of the covenant are secured to us. Outside their ministrations (says each priesthood in turn) all is uncertain. Such or something like it, is the idea on which every priesthood has been based. In addition to this the Catholic priest has the perfectly distinct value of the Christian moralist, and it is the possession of this ethical quality, in addition to the common ground of all priesthoods, that gives its special note, we may add, its special vigour to the hierarchy of the Church. For those who are susceptible to the attraction of a positive religion, who are possible clients of a priesthood, may be roughly divided into two classes. There are those who are most interested in the idea underlying all priesthoods, namely the notion of some certain channel of communication with the unknown. Such as these will thrill with atavistic terrors at the thought of death; they have perhaps done much that they would have undone, and they feel that no natural force exists which can do that for them. The claim of the Catholic priest to do just this—definitely, positively to forgive their sins at a given moment, and thereby ultimately secure them from the terrors of the grave,—is exactly what they want. They do not feel any great interest in the moral or spiritual process implied, still they wind themselves up to it under their confessor's direction, as a necessary condition of what they must have. There are others who are primarily drawn to the ideal life of the Church. Rightly or wrongly they think that that life is the exclusive possession of the Catholic religion. To secure those elements of peace and holiness they are quite willing to fulfil the conditions of membership imposed. So they accept without much thought, or any particular interest in the points involved, the thaumaturgic side of the system. Thus the net of the Kingdom of Heaven takes fish of more than one sort.

If the Catholic priest were merely a priest he would not appeal to these more spiritually-minded clients; if he were merely a moralist he would have no power over the superstitious sin-stricken multitude. As it is, he has the power of holding them both. In order to do this, however, he must do more than advance his claim; he must present himself plausibly in both his capacities. To achieve their combination in one individual an altogether special system of education is necessary, which inevitably results in the formation of a very special and peculiar character. It is this priestly character which is the subject of Fabre's studies, whether he lingers with the country *curés* in the Cévennes, among priests of the Lord who heal the physical ailments of horse and man, as in the *Courbezons* and *Mon Oncle Célestin*, or guides us through the intricacies of the conflict between Rome backed by the religious congregations and the remnants of Gallicanism as in Lucifer, or depicts the terrific shapes which egotism and envy take on in the narrow and darkened soul of an ambitious cleric as in *L'Abbé Tigrane.*

It is a character which fascinates and repels. The narrowness which is the condition of its strength makes it hard of comprehension by the modern world. This fact does not in the least disconcert the priest. 'Dieu a maudit le monde, nous n'avons qu'un devoir stricte envers lui, c'est de le sauver,' says the Superior of the Capuchins in *L'Abbé Tigrane.*

This is no pulpit rhetoric, it represents the sober and permanent conviction of the ecclesiastical conscience, the true 'power behind the Pope.' It is, moreover, the correct deduction from the principles on which that conscience has been formed. From the age of fourteen the future priest is trained in the monastic seclusion of the seminary. That training is of course primarily theological; but theology alone will not fit him for his career as a fisher of men. He must have some notion of history, for history is a part of apologetics; he must know some natural science, for we live in the days of the professor; he must at least have a smattering of philosophy, for Kant and Hegel require periodic refutation. None of these things indeed need he know *for their own sake.* Everything must be done *Ad majorem Dei Gloriam*, and the glory of God is the triumph of the Church. In the ordinary life of men in the 'world,' the ideal motive is intermittent. It intervenes in the play of passion and impulse to correct, to guide, to modify; nor is this state of things without justification. Vauvenargues says that we perhaps owe the greatest advantages of the spirit to our passions, and that, without them, man would never have learned the lesson of reason. Far otherwise is the ecclesiastical view based on a scholastic realism which considers reason and passion not as psychological products, as resultants of the interplay of consciousness and environment, as complementary factors, to be allowed their full value in the construction of character, but as objective entities really existing in the terms of their definitions and necessarily at perpetual war. Hence it comes about that, in the case of the priest, the action of the ideal motive is incessant, omnipresent, all-devouring. Sometimes of course a terrific reaction ensues. Sometimes the strings screwed up to their top note will snap. When this happens, when the priest 'falls,' great indeed is his fall. He is unlikely to stop in his downward course at the average moral or immoral level of the mere man of the world.

The positive elements of the seminary training are reinforced and intensified by the negative. The young Levite is kept in as complete seclusion as possible throughout the whole period of his education. The result is that he grows up in complete ignorance of the real life of men and women in the world. He has no conception of the existence of any ethical system whatever except the one in which he has been trained. All those then who do not acknowledge the claims of that system are necessarily without real morality. Matthew Arnold has told us in one of his most charming essays, of the account of the religion of Paganism which he found in the Abbé Migne's *Dictionnaire des Origines du Christianisme.* 'Paganism invented a mob of divinities with the most hateful character, and attributed to them the most monstrous and abominable crimes. It personified in them drunkenness, incest, kidnapping, adultery, sensuality, knavery, cruelty and rage . . . what must naturally have been the state of morals under the influence of such a religion, which penetrated with its own spirit the public life, the family life, and the individual life of antiquity.' Scarcely less wide of the mark is the only view of the world around him possible to the average seminarist. What can the noblest aspirations of modern life be to him? Mere *deliramenta.* What can he think of the passion of liberty when he has been taught to believe that all ethic is founded on the basic virtue of minute and rigid obediencc to authority? What he thinks of the desire for justice, so ineradicable an element of the modern conscience, the last few years of French history have proved us *ad nauseam.*

Thus armed with weapons which, if they were adapted for the purpose in hand, he would lack the strength to wield, he emerges at the age of twenty-four to do battle with a world which, even in the countries in which he stands without serious rivals as the representative of the religious principle, needs the stimulus of an electoral crisis seriously to advert to his existence. He soon finds that the sword which flashed so bravely in the mimic warfare of seminary dialectics, snaps in his hand like a stage-property when employed on the actualities of life; that men have grown hopelessly suspicious of

> The old-world cures they half believe
> For woes they wholly understand.

Then one of two things happens. If he be a man of naturally indolent character he retires into his presbytery as a snail into his shell. Those who want him can seek him out. He knows that the world is all wrong. 'Totus mundus in maligno positus est,' says the Apostle, but he lacks the strength and perseverance to keep on crying the melancholy fact into deaf ears in the market-place. To what end indeed? No one listens to him. Not for nothing has he put off the 'old man' of his secular garments and been clothed in the *angelica vestis* of the 'new.' He has lost his old, his human self, and has put on the abstract personality of the Church, and it is just that personality that the world will have none of. He finds himself in the position of having constantly to prove his existence as a preliminary to the securing of a hearing. And the position is an unpleasant, an intolerable one. So he gives it up and retires to lay mines according to his ability. On the other hand, a man of really strong character, whose virility has not been sapped by his training, is stung by his painful position into the extreme of combativeness. The celestial war-cry: *Quis ut Deus!* rings in his ears. God's victory cannot be doubtful and God's victory is the Church's and the Church's is his own. In this way we reach the type of the Abbé Tigrane.

This great man is undoubtedly the most important of Fabre's ecclesiastical creations. Vividly as the others are painted, they pale before his fires. He glows with the flamboyant colours of an Hildebrand or an Innocent III., and, in happier days, his career would doubtless have been such as theirs. As it is we take leave of him an Archbishop, still in the prime of his life, discussing with his faithful Vicar-General his chances of the Cardinalate and the Papacy.

The Abbé Ruffin Capdepont, nicknamed by his companions in the seminary Abbé Tigrane on account of his irritability, is one of the high officials of the diocese of Lormières which is governed at the time the story opens by the aristocratic, generous-minded Mgr. de Roquebrun. This prelate has also his weaknesses of temper which do not make easier his relations with his Supérieur du Grand Séminaire.

Capdepont hates the bishop, who has, he conceives, robbed him of the diocese of Lormières. *Nolo Episcopari* was never his motto, and he had so dwelt on the chances of his appointment to the see that when Mgr. Roquebrun was chosen for the mitre he felt it was a personal and unforgiveable insult.

'On ne sait pas assez chez les laïques ce qu'est l'épiscopat pour un prêtre. Hier vous étiez simple soldat dans une armée de quatre-vingt mille hommes (il y a environ quatre-vingt mille ecclésiastiques en France), aujourd'hui vous passez tout d'un coup général. La transition n'est pas plus ménagée que cela. Le desservant, le curé-doyen, le chanoine, le grand-vicaire possèdent les mêmes droits canoniques restreints; l'évêque seul possède le sacerdoce dans sa plénitude. Et puis quelle situation autre dans le monde! vous êtes prince de la Sainte Eglise Romaine, on vous appelle "Monseigneur," le pape ne vous nomme plus que "Vénérable Frère," s'il veut prononcer une décision relative à la réforme du dogme ou de la discipline il ne peut le faire sans vous; (*L'Abbé Tigrane* was written before 1870) vous allez à Rome, *ad limina apostolorum*, comme on dit, et l'on vous reçoit au Vatican avec la haute distinction accordée aux souverains. Qui sait si maintenant que vous avez la mitre d'évêque, vous n'obtiendrez pas plus tard la barette de Cardinal? Qui sait même si, par le fait des révolutions dont nos temps ne sont pas avares, vous ne coifferez pas un jour la tiare? Urbain IV. n'était-il pas le fils d'un savetier de Troye? Jean XXII. n'avait-il pas vu le jour à Cahors?'

It must not be supposed that the Supérieur du Grand Séminaire is represented as a 'bad priest.' Far from it; his morals are above suspicion; 'Je fus toujours chaste!' he exclaims one day, in a moment of expansion to his confidant l'Abbé Mical. He has but one passion—ambition.

'*Zelus domus tuæ comedit me!*' His zeal for the glory of God's house has turned into a monstrous, despotic egotism. God must conquer; who so fit to win the Church's battle as himself? But, to win that battle, he must have a free hand, he must have power, ever more and more power. He, at last, comes in his monomania to identify himself with his cause, or rather his cause with himself. He can only see the triumph of God in his own exaltation. So he is led, on the occasion of Mgr. de Roquebrun's funeral, into a moment of real insanity, when, to the horror even of his own supporters, he snatches at the episcopal ring on the hand of the deceased prelate, whom he insults in death by refusing admission to his body into his own cathedral. The critics took exception to this terrible scene on the ground of caricature. Fabre replied that the Abbé Tigrane was no fictitious character, and that he had not dared to give the real facts of the case as they had come to his knowledge precisely for fear of that criticism. The original Tigrane had left the Bishop's remains, not in the Cathedral square, but in the episcopal stables!

It is needless to say that Tigrane aspired to succeed the Bishop, and such was his ability that he did so. His enemies did not fail to inform the Vatican of his scandalous behaviour, but in vain.

No one, of course, supposes—Fabre least of all—that Tigrane is the average priest. He is typical in a very different sense to that. All strong-minded men of action are inclined to be ambitious, and their ambition may, as likely as not, assume a form which is profitable to society. In Tigrane we see an extreme instance of the ravages of ambition in the ecclesiastical soul. And precisely that form of ambition is essentially a priestly vice—or virtue. Its peculiar quality as well as its intensity comes from the identification by the priest of himself with the Highest, of his own egotism with the transcendental egotism of the Church. It is in the fact that no one but he is in the position to make that identification, that the unique quality of the priest's ambition consists, while its peculiar intensity is due to the concentration of his professional ideal of all that energy which, in the case of most men, is distributed over a variety of objects, together with the narrowness of outlet which is the inevitable result of his education. No one knew better than Fabre that all priests are not ambitious, and, in his long series of ecclesiastical portraits, he has shown us not a few humble and zealous servants of humanity. To them all honour. But he has shown us in Tigrane a typical instance of what clerical ambition means, and he also knew how liable priests are to that particular vice. The drunken or incontinent priest is the victim of faults common to all men. Such a one *pecca come uomo*—he sins as a man—as a dignitary once said to the present writer: Tigrane, on the other hand, may be said to sin as Lucifer.

In reading these criticisms of the French and English Churches one cannot but be struck by the difference of the problems presented by either form of Christianity. The anonymous forces which, by their more or less constant equilibrium, have maintained the Church of England in existence, must necessarily come under the influence of the Time-spirit. Indeed, it is obvious that that spirit is what gives the Church its 'form,' as scholastics would say; while, on the other hand, the Catholic Church anathematises, in Pius IX.'s Syllabus, those who would be rash enough to maintain 'that the Roman Pontiff can and ought to effect a reconciliation and compromise with progress, liberalism, and modern civilisation.' And though ecclesiastical authority has at present a wary course to steer between the achieved results of secular science and the positions to which traditional theology stands committed, its success is not by any means so uncertain as anti-clericals like to think. For those positions by no means always engage infallibility, and, even when they do, the infallibility of a decree is one thing, and its interpretation another. Interpretation may well be progressive. This is not the place to discuss the ecclesiastical future of Europe, but I may be allowed at the close of this essay to indicate an element of the discussion which too often fails to obtain recognition. The real life of the Catholic Church is its mystical life. The Church's politico-ecclesiastical appearance shifts and changes, it is the work of men not, as a rule, distinguished above their fellows for intelligence or spiritual quality, and often conspicuously below them. To suppose that the life of the Church depends on anything they can say or do would be a grotesque inversion of things. The sources of the Church's life are not to be found in consistories or any conceivable priestly conciliabule, but are deep in the semi-conscious soul of the civilisation at whose birth she was present and to whose development her assistance has, up till our day, been necessary. Will that assistance be always necessary? or, to vary the question, will those sources ever run dry? He would be a rash man who would answer.

JORIS-KARL HUYSMANS

SIXTEEN years ago M. Jules Huret, the well-known Parisian journalist, published an *Enquête sur l'Évolution Littéraire.* He interviewed some thirty of the best-known novelists and men of letters in France and gave their views to the world without comment, save that involved in the colloquial skill with which he gracefully delivered them of their opinions. And he thus produced a most interesting and important volume. Apart from the literary value of the pot-pourri, its significance was of the highest. For the writers interviewed—such was M. Huret's professional ability—did not hesitate to express themselves with ingenuous candour on their own prospects and those of their *confrères.*

On first reading one derived but a hopelessly confused impression, but gradually, as the cloud of stormy eloquence rose, one discerned two things on which the writers interviewed seemed pretty well agreed: That naturalism was dead, and that among the *jeunes,* from whom something new was to be expected, Huysmans, Remy de Gourmont, and Maurice Barrès had, in the vivid vernacular of the French writing-table, *quelque chose dans le ventre.* Sixteen years have passed, and Barrès has left the battles of letters for the repose of the Palais Bourbon and the Academy, Remy de Gourmont has produced several volumes of philosophical romance of a high order, and continues to delight us twice a month in the *Mercure de France* with his own strongly individualised blend of Nietzsche and Renan, while Huysmans has left us for ever within the last few months. He entered into peace through the gate of pain, of pain so intolerable that it will not bear thinking of, but before the eyes of that lover of exquisite sensation were veiled by his last unutterable anguish, he had accomplished his task.

Joris-Karl Huysmans, who was born in Paris of Flemish descent, in 1848, commenced author as a fervent disciple of Zola. He was one of the contributors to the famous *Soirées de Medan* with *Sac-à-dos*, a masterpiece of ferocious irony, in which the real distress of the patriotic conscript is not caused by the heroic sufferings of war, but by an unintermittent colic. The satire of the little tale is Rabelaisian both in its intensity and the coarseness of its detail, and its essential irony is enhanced by its humbling and brutal verisimilitude. We cannot doubt, as we lay it down, that this, or something like it is, in fact, what war means to most of the obscure thousands who are sacrificed to its lurid prestige and dubious benefits. I do not know whether anarchists make use of *Sac-à-dos* for their propaganda; they certainly could not do better. *Les Sœurs Vatard,* published in 1879, and dedicated to Zola by 'his fervent admirer and devoted Friend,' is, however, the greatest work produced by Huysmans, during what is called his naturalist period. It is indeed one of the finest works produced by any of the writers of that school, and far more faithful to the naturalist formula than Zola's epic poems in prose. Huysmans understood naturalism in the sense of Flaubert, who, in spite of the romantic beauty of his expression, revealed himself as the first and greatest of the naturalists in *Mme. Bovary.* Huysmans indeed renounced, whether unconsciously, or through deliberate reflection, Flaubert's search for beauty of expression, seeking nothing but accuracy and fulness of presentation. This he achieves by means of an amazing accumulation of physical detail, which produces on the imagination almost the effect of an actual experience. There is a description of a Fair in *Les Sœurs Vatard,* which is one of the most astonishing pieces of realistic writing ever composed. As you read it the book fades before your eyes: you are there, at Vincennes, you are burnt by the sun, you are deafened by the shouts of cheap-jacks, you eagerly elbow your way through the steaming, struggling crowd to contemplate the charms of the *femme colosse* and the sinister arts of the serpent-charmer; you are alternately touched and mortified by the sentimental gaucheries of Désirée Vatard, who clings after the manner of her class to your arm, and when you lay the book down, you feel the physical and mental fatigue inseparable from such a way of passing the afternoon. In this book Huysmans succeeds in transferring, by suggestion, sensorial impressions to the imagination directly, with all the acute crudeness of sheer physical contact. But this is not all. The psychology of Désirée and Céline Vatard, the wise and the foolish virgin, is presented carefully and convincingly. Two years out of the lives of two little Parisian work-girls, one of whom is temperamentally chaste and the other the reverse, but both of them *bonnes filles*, Céline the *noceuse*, with a highly comical sense of her own dignity and her soul of a poor little animal which, after all, asks only to gratify its instincts; Désirée, the virtuous, with all the elements of the *jeune fille* of bourgeois romance, saved from her sister's troubles by a natural modesty of blood, as primary and ineluctable a necessity of her being, as Céline's riotous desires are of hers—this is all the story. And yet on this narrow scene, within these sordid and trivial limits, the whole of life seems to pass before us. The ambitious generalisation, the pseudo-scientific theorising of Zola, is wholly absent from the pages. Every character in the pitiful little play from the leading ladies to the merest super, to the strangers one brushes in the street, is individualised, is given his full value as a human unique, every episode is made wholly concrete, the author not only never once betrays any desire to explain things, but does not even suggest the faintest personal interest in his puppets. He is wholly absent from his creation, his pen seeming to react mechanically to the stimulus of the spectacle. Flaubert's ideal of the impersonality of the artist is attained, and the effect is the most poignant imaginable. Just so, we feel, would life appear to us if we saw it as it really is, apart from the deforming mirage of our egoistic passions. Just so would it appear, we think, to some superhuman intelligence, some angel or demi-urge who, freed from the limitations and exigencies of sense perception, would be equally emancipated from those torturing and delicious derivatives of the senses, the imagination and the emotions. But, after all, such a fantastic hypothesis is unnecessary, it is just so that it appears to the purified eye of the scientific observer 'from hope and fear set free.'

Equally galling to the vital instinct and satisfactory to the instinct of knowledge is *A Vau l'Eau.* It is a short story of some fifteen thousand words which details the miseries of a *vieux célibataire* in Paris. M. Folantin is a Government *employé* at £60 a year; he is timid in temperament, moderate in desires, but he possesses a plain, strong intelligence which precludes the possibility of contentment with the few poor illusions which his pittance can buy. Once more, in this dreary little tale, we are made to drink the bitter lees of existence. The essential bitterness of the draught is caused by the absolute futility of such lives as M. Folantin's. And millions of such lives are necessitated by the conditions of humanity. It is not merely that all super-terrestrial hope, all religious and metaphysical aspiration are banished from such lives—this if we accept science as our only reliable guide, we must be prepared for—it is that such lives themselves are hopelessly mutilated. It is, however, in the conviction of the nothingness, the *néant* of life, that Huysmans finds the real tragedy of humanity. It is not merely that men suffer—the highest hope that ever irradiated man's heart was based on the joyous acceptance of suffering—it is that neither suffering nor joy really matter. The universe goes on its senseless way to its purposeless end that is no conclusion—for it never ends, or rather it ends but to re-commence—blindly throwing up from the depths of the unconscious, millions of conscious organisms, stamped as, under the old régime, French criminals were branded with a red-hot fleur de lys, with the ironic insignia of an illusory royalty. Man waves his stage sceptre with an inalienable sense of freedom and power, and what happens? That which was irrevocably determined to happen when our solar system was still but a nebula, but a faintly luminous corona in the ether. And the irony of the situation is raised to its highest, most sinister point when we reflect that man's illusion is as surely determined as his impotence. For what is 'man's place in the universe'? For a few seconds the world reaches the point of self-consciousness, and mirrors itself in the passive contemplation of a human mind before sinking again into the unconscious eternity on the surface of which organic life itself is but a ripple. Those minds are re-duplicated a millionfold, yet each subsists but for a few moments while, sooner or later, the conditions of the planet will no longer permit the existence of any at all.

As the conditions of life burn lower the universe will slowly turn from the enigmatic and redoubtable experiment of self-consciousness, and the peace of death will brood once more over unconscious matter. Such is the world as known to naturalism, and the contemplation of it as the only certitude bred in Huysmans a dull despair. He exhaled his hatred of life in that strange fantasy *A Rebours*. Life is worthless indeed, but, for the privileged few, there is art. Let us then abandon life and live in an aristocratic dream of beauty, of beauty created by our own brains and hands, for the so-called beauty of nature is a delusion. The beauty of nature lends directly or indirectly to the strengthening and enhancing of the vital instinct, and therefore to the perpetuation of the iniquity of life. Nature's appeal is so obviously in most cases to the nerves rather than to the brain, hence the success of the uneducated. Popular 'art' follows also the line of least resistance, there must be something wrong even about Rembrandt, for such hopeless people admire him. He might have added that moonlight cannot really be beautiful because it makes nurse-maids sentimental.

The further art can go from nature the better. The artistic sensations that Huysmans preferred were subtle, rare and complex. The Art that is simple and majestic, the Art, for instance, that was the product of the Greek mind, says nothing to him. The neurotic hero, Des Esseintes, who has retired to the hermitage of his villa to live a life of delicate inversion, spends an hour or two dreaming over his favourite books. His 'Index' is significant. Virgil is 'L'un des plus terribles cuistres, l'un des plus sinistres raseurs que l'antiquité ait jamais produits.' Horace 'a des grâces éléphantines.' Ovid and Tacitus bore him less than other classical writers, but he is really at his ease only with the Decadents. Lucan and Petronius ravish him, particularly Petronius in his *Satyricon.* At the end of the book Des Esseintes feels the reminiscent sting of his early religious training and cries aloud for Faith. The book closes with his prayer: 'Seigneur, prenez pitié du chrétien qui doute, de l'incrédule qui voudrait croire, du forçat de la vie qui s'embarque seul, dans la nuit sous un firmament que n'éclairent plus les consolants fanaux du vieil espoir!' This monograph on æsthetic neurasthenia, as it might be called, contains some of the finest passages Huysmans ever wrote. Take the marvellous description of Gustave Moreau's *l'Apparition* or Des Esseintes' terrific vision of Scrofula, the secular scourge of human generations. Never have words been made to do so much. *A Rebours*, opening with Des Esseintes' rejection of life, and ending with his hysterical cry for Faith, is the bridge connecting Huysmans' first and second period; his naturalism and his mysticism. Yet this criticism, in order not to be misleading, must be made more precise. In method Huysmans remained an impenitent naturalist to the end. Whether he is writing of M. Folantin's despairing hunt for a decent meal in the restaurants of his *quartier*, or of the visions of St. Lidwina of Schiedam, his methods are always the same. He proceeds invariably by the accumulation of physical details which build up, as it were, cell by cell, the organic whole of the scene he is evoking. The intensity of the evocation, when complete, is due to the power with which the details are made to live in themselves, and the skill with which they are inter-related. He produces a composition which lives in the apparently spontaneous unity of a concrete moment. For—and in an attempt to appreciate Huysmans, the point cannot be too strongly made,—he is always concerned with the concrete episode, which is indeed what gives him his place among the purest and greatest of naturalistic Masters, affiliating him also, in no uncertain way, to those other great naturalist artists, the painters of his native land. The technique of his imaginative perception is very closely reminiscent of the methods of the Flemish painters. The exquisite conscientiousness with which his details are finished, his sense of colour, a certain rich simplicity of order in his composition, the constant recurrence of certain elements—meals almost taking the place in his pages of the white horse with his red-coated rider in the pictures of

Wouvermans—his sense for the sordid, the trivial, are characteristics which surely indicate the artistic family to which he belongs.

In discourse he is at his worst. The theological and archæological disquisitions which seem to be interpolated, as indeed they are, in his later works, have a merely informational value and that, I fancy, not always of the soundest. Certainly his theology sounds peculiar at times. Nor does their weakness come from the inherent difficulty in taking up a new subject in middle age: it comes from his innate incapacity to express himself in the way of discourse. His attempts at reasoning in *Les Foules de Lourdes*, one of his latest works in which he hotly defends the miraculous nature of that successful watering-place, are those of a clever child who constantly misses the point through his inability to resist distractions. You feel too that he is aware of his unconvincingness, and being unable, from the nature of the case, to use his own methods, turns in vain to bitterness and even, on occasion, to personal abuse of those so unfortunate as not to share his prepossessions, in order, as they say, to help himself out. The same tendency is visible in the didactic parts of *En Route*.

We have seen that there is no difference in Huysmans' earlier and later methods, that his change was not in manner but in content. In the first pages of *Là-Bas*, the volume which follows *A Rebours* and precedes *En Route*, there occurs a dialogue which throws a light on his new departure. After Des Hermies has said that naturalism was the incarnation of materialism in literature, the glorification of democracy in art, so correct a representation of bourgeois ideas, 'qu'il semble une parole, issue de l'accouplement de Lisa, la charcutière du Ventre de Paris et de Homais,' Durtal replies: 'Le matérialisme me répugne tout autant qu'à toi, mais ce n'est pas une raison pour nier les inoubliables services que les naturalistes ont rendus à l'art, car, enfin, ce sont eux qui nous ont débarassés des inhumains fantoches du romantisme et qui ont extrait la littérature d'une idéalisme de ganache et d'une inanition de vieille fille exaltée par le célibat! En somme, après Balzac, ils ont créé des êtres visibles et palpables et ils les ont mis en accord avec leurs alentours, ils ont aidé au développement de la langue commencée par les romantiques; ils ont connu le véritable rire et ont parfois même le don des larmes, enfin, ils n'ont pas toujours été soulevés par ce fanatisme de bassesse dont tu parles.'

Des Hermies leaves and Durtal continues his soliloquy, summing up his conclusions as follows:—'Il faudrait garder la véracité du document, la précision du detail, la langue étoffée et nerveuse du réalisme, mais il faudrait aussi se faire puisatier d'âme et ne pas vouloir expliquer le mystère par les maladies des sens; le roman, si cela se pouvait, devrait se deviser de lui-même en deux parts, néanmoins soudées ou plutôt confondues, comme elles le sont dans la vie, celle de l'âme, celle du corps, et s'occuper de leurs réactifs, de leurs conflits, de leur entente. Il faudrait, en un mot, suivre la grande voie si profondément creusée par Zola, mais il serait nécessaire aussi de tracer en l'air un chemin parallèle, une autre route, d'atteindre les en deça et les après, de faire, en un mot, un naturalisme spiritualiste; ce serait autrement fier, autrement complet, autrement fort!'

Such is the artistic programme which Huysmans attempted to carry out in his later period. As I have said, he in no way wished to modify the methods of his technique which remained essentially naturalist; he wished to enlarge the content of his art, to widen the field of his observation. When he speaks of tracing in the air a parallel line to Zola's line of physical observation he makes indeed a philosophical advance on his former position, for sound philosophy recognises that experience needs for its constitution a subject as well as an object, from which it follows that a state of mind as such, independently of its physical accompaniment, is as truly a fact as a state of body. This step was no doubt taken unconsciously, for there never was a mind more radically incapable of any kind of philosophic speculation than his. It is nevertheless what constitutes the human interest of the work of his later period. For that interest certainly cannot be said to lie in his somewhat bizarre presentation of Christian mythology, which he happened to find ready to his hand, to be tortured and inverted by the horrible maniacs whom he shows us in *Là-Bas*, to be enthusiastically, if somewhat uncritically, glorified in *En Route* and his other distinctively Catholic works. It lies surely in the recognition of the mystery of human experience diffused through these volumes, together with the sense of pity of the human lot and of the supreme value of love. For these emotions he found both adequate expression and an adequate stimulus, in the symbols of mediæval mysticism. Nor was that expression and that stimulus purely literary. As is known, the road of Damascus, on which Durtal travels from *Là-Bas* to *L'Oblat*, was the path followed by his creator. Whether Huysmans' interest in Catholicism was due in the first instance to the exigencies of his literary development or to the necessities of his soul is an unprofitable subject of inquiry. It is enough for the critic to note that his hand grew subdued to what he worked in, and that the man came to acquiesce, with the full fervour of intense conviction, in the doctrines of the writer. To criticise the personal solution in which he at length found peace would be foreign to the subject of this essay, and obviously of the nature of an impertinence. Nevertheless as there have been several, and not of one camp only, who have openly expressed their doubts of the sincerity of his attitude, I cannot refrain from expressing the opinion that never was there a more complete, a more sincere conversion than that of Huysmans. None of the psychological elements of such a change were wanting to him. A disgust of contemporary life and an invincible repulsion to its ideals, together with an ardent attraction for the naïve beauty of the mediæval soul, for the whole domain of that wondrous 'fief of Art,' as he calls it, which was the creation of the mediæval Church—these were most prominent among the *raisons de cœur* which prevailed with him. The mysterious crystallisation of these elements into the definite attitude of belief, is as necessarily beyond criticism as any other vital phenomenon. So much may perhaps be said without offence. When, however, we turn to the literary expression of his convictions, we are once more in the world of discourse, we have once more before us matter for reasoned appreciation. What cannot fail to strike any one at all familiar with contemporary Catholic literature is that Huysmans' religious books fall into a category of their own. The man submits to the discipline which is to save his soul, the writer remains a free lance. The distinctive Catholic literature of our day is either apologetic or written for purposes of edification. And the public which it is attempted to edify must be confined entirely, one would think, to women and children. Huysmans certainly did not try to put himself in line with this class of book. And, as regards apologetic, it must be admitted that so far as he had it in mind at all, it was of a very different kind to that which we associate with the subtle disquisitions of philosophers, such as Laberthonnière and Leroy, or the quasi-socialist propaganda of the Christian democrats. The social or philosophical possibilities of present-day religion had not the slightest interest for his mind which was spellbound by the vision of the glorious past, *le moyen âge énorme et délicat.* In fact he was a mediævalist before he was a Catholic. In *Là-Bas*, while still far from any mental state which could be called faith, he is a firm believer in the supernatural, in magic, black and white. He knows the names of many demons and their functions in the cosmic economy. Indeed it is matter of reproach with him against the ecclesiastical authorities, that they betray so languid an interest in demonology; are, in fact, as he fears, tainted with scepticism.

Why insist on trying to come to an understanding with M. Clémenceau, when you are really dealing with Azrael?

Thus he resuscitates for us in his vibrant pages that old world, and makes it live once more with its fantastic hopes and fears, its heaven and hell, its angels and saints and demons. He does more. He resuscitates also its beauty. The guardians of the heavenly city to-day are often too much absorbed in the immediate exigencies of the Holy War to care for the beauty of the streets of Jerusalem. The service which Huysmans has done in calling attention to the treasure of Art which is the heritage of the Catholic Church is one which should make the members of that Church his debtors, and in any case, entitles him to the gratitude of all lovers of the beautiful everywhere.

MAETERLINCK

Among contemporary masters of prose, no one, I think, gives so unique an impression, no one exhales so special a fragrance as Maeterlinck. Is he a lyric poet? Is he a dramatist? Is he a moralist? It is hard to say; indeed, he seems to be all of these by turn, and, even, on occasion, at once.

He has written many miniature dramas—'Shakespeare for Marionettes,' he calls them himself—some of which are the most poignant little pieces imaginable, all drenched with the tears and mystery of things; fragments of life itself, we think, as we read or watch them for the first time, almost catching our breath at the naïveté of their frankness, at their childlike ingenuousness. He has signed pages of criticism, in their way inimitable; although they do not contain much of what is ordinarily understood by the term. His essays on Emerson, Ruysbroeck, and Novalis convey no personal impression whatever of those great ones; they deal with the pure idea, and barely advert to the human envelope. But then the idea is made to thrill with a mystic personality, more intense than any which could be suggested by the greatest accumulation of circumstantial or merely casual detail. Such work is at the opposite pole of the critical art to, say, Mr. Gosse's admirable study of Coventry Patmore. There, bit by bit, the human being is reconstructed and presented to us with all the illusion of a live-eyed portrait, as he was seen, loved and hated by his contemporaries. It is just this suggestion of familiarity, of personal knowledge, so skilfully conveyed by the art of Mr. Gosse, which is utterly lacking to the essays of Maeterlinck. From his point of view, such treatment would be worse than irrelevant: it would be almost indecent. On that high tableland of the spirit, against the background of those eternal snows, the human gesture, which our flesh cannot but love, would pathetically dwindle into a grotesque and pitiful pantomime.

It is said that some of the most beautiful effects of Corot's landscapes were produced by the master at such a distance from the subject he was painting that all detail was indistinguishable to the eye. So Maeterlinck discerns the spiritual values of a Novalis or a Ruysbroeck by altogether overlooking their existence in time and space, and concentrating his gaze on the light of the idea which they at once conceal and manifest. For if, to the winking eyes of most of us, that light is only tolerable by being broken on the prism, as it were, of the seer's personality, by being refracted through the daily habit of his life and conversation, which thus reveals to us as much of it as we can bear, all that to Maeterlinck does but conceal what he is in search of. He prefers to look straight at the sun. We, who are not eagles, suffer in the effort to share his vision; and a darkness, which we feel would reveal so much could we but pierce it, is apt to descend on our straining gaze. The same criticism applies to the other essays—on moral and spiritual subjects—collected in the same volume under the title of *Le Trésor des Humbles*. Here and there the clouds part, and an astonishingly pure and lambent ray gladdens us for a moment; we feel we never knew what light was before, like those who for the first time see the Italian sun; then, once more, obscurity. One thing, however, no conscientious student of Maeterlinck can maintain; and that is, that his obscurity partakes in ever so slight a degree of a pose, of a deliberate mystification. Here is no attitude of indifference, no mask of intellectual scorn, but rather the patient effort of a most unusual sincerity which, with the obvious repression of a fine rhetorical gift, endeavours to express exactly what is meant; just that and nothing more. Such sincerity inevitably appears a little forced and artificial to those who come to it fresh from the comfortable atmosphere of polite human intercourse. Professor Wallace attributes the difficulty presented by Hegel's philosophy to a beginner, to the contrast which it offers to our ordinary habits of mind. 'Generally speaking, we rest contented if we can get tolerably near our object, and form a general picture of it to set before ourselves. It might almost be said that we have never thought of such a thing as being in earnest, either with our words or with our thoughts.' Just such a contrast exists between our habitual retailing, for purposes of social currency, of our profoundest and most intimate emotions, and Maeterlinck's method of dealing with them. We cannot avoid the prick, that if we were purer in heart, we should understand him better.

It is proposed here to consider Maeterlinck as a moralist. That the preoccupation of morals, of the practical art of life, has always been with him, is evident; in his earliest work it is not absent, but it has only disengaged itself and become fully self-conscious in his latest writings, in *La Sagesse et la Destinée*, *Le Temple Ensveli*, and *Le Double Jardin*; and it will be with these volumes that we shall be here principally concerned. It may, however, be well, before considering their contents, to have clearly before us the state of mind to which Maeterlinck addresses himself. The condition of the hearer is always an important part of the message he receives; and this is especially so when the teacher, as in the present instance, is rather a master of suggestion than of exposition. What then is the mental attitude on this subject of his readers, so numerous and appreciative that a new 'Maeterlinck' has no sooner appeared than it has flown in its thousands over Europe?

'Nous sortons de la grande période religieuse.' That great change, gradually produced during the last three hundred years in European opinion, which has reduced theology from the position of the Queen of the Sciences to the rank of an individual and private speculation, has had its repercussion in other departments of inquiry than the theological. Indeed it would not be hard to show that no branch whatever of human knowledge has remained unaffected by it. Based itself in its origin on knowledge of a particular kind, it has succeeded in extending its 'sphere of influence' over much which might seem foreign to it. The discovery of Copernicus was more than a celestial *coup d'État*. It did more than overthrow man's sovereignty of the heavens ; it surely numbered the days of Theocracy on earth. That revolution of humanity on its own axis which has produced the Arts, the State, Religion and Morality, could not remain unaffected by it. Nor has it done so. Slowly but surely, what is called the scientific spirit has taken over every part of human experience.

A phrase like 'the scientific spirit' is apt to become a catchword. What precisely do we mean by it? Well, I suppose we mean the habit of mind engendered by familiarity with the method, even if not with the achievements, of exact knowledge. It is not necessary, in order to possess it, to know the secrets of the laboratory or the test tube; but we shall not gain it if we do not understand the principle on which those secrets are discovered. That principle is belief in the unity and intelligibility in terms of relatedness, of the whole phenomenal universe, from which it results that a hypothesis has scientific value, in proportion to its success in co-ordinating the group of phenomena with which it deals, thus tending towards that ideal unity, which it is the aim of science as a whole to attain. The metaphysician will tell us that this belief is a mere assumption; and so, in the terms of his art, it is. But it is the assumption which underlies all possibility of any knowledge which is to be more than mere random and, occasionally, happy guess-work. For science is no esoteric craft. The physiologist or the chemist has no short cut to truth; he uses precisely the same faculties of perception and ratiocination by means of which we all organise a journey from Victoria to the Gare du Nord. He uses them no doubt with far greater caution, with an infinitely nicer sense of what is meant by evidence, of the exigencies of demonstration, than the layman; but his instrument of investigation differs only in degree of precision. It is an ill-judged contempt that some people pour on popular science; if science were not, at least potentially, popular, it would not be science at all. Of course, pure, as distinguished from applied, science does require certain special habits of trained attention which are not at the command of all of us. But the most advanced scientific experimentalist has no other faculties to use in his investigations than those which lie more or less idle in the brains of all of us. Once stated, this is obvious; but it is by no means so universally appreciated as might be thought. Many educated people talk of science as if it were a special department of knowledge, or one particular way of knowing things; whereas, in truth, the only real knowledge is scientific knowledge.

Another fallacy, common enough among the laity, is to confuse the method of science in general with the results of any particular science. Thus the champions of intellectual reaction not infrequently argue from the errors which inevitably attach to those results, to the discredit of the idea of science itself. 'How little, after all, we know,' they say, 'and how unreliable that little! Science shifts like the sand; how can we take it seriously?' These critics do not realise the distinction between the method of science and its results in application. They do not see that it is by clinging more and more faithfully to that method, that the results are gradually and progressively made perfect, that any stage of investigation must, as such, be defective, and finally that, however unreliable and scanty scientific results at any moment may be, they represent at that moment the state of our knowledge on that subject, and form themselves the point of departure for further development. No one knew better the defects of his hypothesis than Darwin; and it is just those defects that have been so fruitful in the further development of his science. There are many, however, and they are a daily increasing number, who realise that, in the method of science, man has discovered the true law of his knowledge; and it is they who dwell in the mental atmosphere of the scientific spirit. This atmosphere it is, rather than the negative arguments derivable from any particular branch of science, that has produced the effect on theological belief alluded to above; and it has produced it largely through the change in the conception of truth which it implies. In pre-scientific days, truth was any desirable opinion which could not be disproved; now the quality of truth attaching to a statement is felt to be in exact ratio to the evidence producible for it.

The weakening of theological belief has not been without its effect upon morals. In the theological period, by which I mean the period during which theology was universally accepted by us Westerns as the basis of human existence (controversy turning only on which was in fact the true theology), morality was heteronomous, being based on the will of God revealed to man *ab extra*. That it possessed an intrinsic value was not denied except by a few mystics; but its mode of presentation was authoritative or external, among Protestants and Catholics alike. It was held that the conscience, rightly directed and illuminated, would indeed recognise the moral quality of the Divine law, but that it would recognise it as such, rather than as the externalisation of the immanent law of its own being. Such recognition involved many non-moral elements, such as particular judgments of fact—that this revelation and not another was the true one

—or a philosophical judgment that Monotheism, rather than Pantheism or Atheism, was the ultimate truth of things. In proportion as the grounds for either or both of these judgments were felt to give way under critical analysis, the heteronomous sanction of morality disappeared. To the minds of many to-day, judgments of either kind appear not so much erroneous as gratuitous and illegitimate; and it is to such, and such only, that Maeterlinck addresses himself.

This emancipation of morality has seemed to many a great and glorious thing; and so it may be. Nevertheless it cannot, I think, be denied that the transition of the art of conduct from heteronomy to autonomy is attended with some danger to the content of morality—to our material if not to our formal virtue. Many delicate readjustments are required, if the passage from the service of God to the service of man is to be effected without loss by the way. The issue is not quite fairly put by those who see in the doctrine of personal rewards and punishments the sole value of the theological sanction of human conduct. It was more, it was other than merely this. That sanction amounted to a popular and dramatic representation of the belief that Man was, in fact, the most important part of the universe, and his conscience the most important part of Man. It implied that Man touched the deepest reality in his conscience only: the universe else was illusion. The triumph of good in the long run was certain; the victory of evil, so palpable and evident, but a shadow that would flee away at the moment of dayspring, when the Sun of Righteousness would disperse the darkness and consummate in the blaze of absolute justice the drama of humanity. The Infinite was consciously on the side of the human soul which was fashioned in its image.

Now all this is changed. 'It is incomparably more probable that the Invisible and the Infinite intervene at every moment in our life under the form of indifferent, enormous, blind elements, which pass over and within us, penetrating, shaping and animating us, without suspecting our existence, as do water, fire, air and light. Now the whole of our conscious life, all this life which constitutes our one certitude and our one fixed point in time and space, reposes in the last resort on incomparable probabilities of the same order; and it is rare that they are so incomparable as these.' In these words Maeterlinck resumes for us the moral sanction of science. And yet, as he adds: 'The whole of our moral organism is made to live in justice, as our physical organism is made to live in the atmosphere of our globe.' Thus a seemingly absolute dilemma is created, in which what ought to be is at hopeless variance with what is. It is not merely that the universe is not what we wish it were; it is, and this is very different, that it is not what we judge it ought to be.

There are various ways of meeting this situation. There is the way of heroic pessimism, which has found a noble expression in the Buddhist rhapsodies of the French poet-philosopher Jean Lahor. There is the attitude of mingled pity and irony which we associate with the best work of Anatole France. There is the immoralism of Nietzsche, echoed by many thoughtless persons, who would shudder at the self-discipline which it involves. Maeterlinck takes none of these ways. It must be confessed that he does not attempt any dogmatic solution, nor does he even allude, in passing, to those suggested by others. He is content to observe directly, for himself, the moral phenomenon with the grave, wide-eyed gaze of an inspired child. In his two latest books, the metaphysical preoccupations observable in his earlier work seem to have dropped off him. Life, the actual tale of days of men and women, working in fields and cities, in courts and camps, at home and abroad, 'on perilous seas forlorn,' has laid on him the fascination of its touch. It is in this actuality, this nearness to experience, that his value consists. He probes into the moral fact as we find it in our common human nature, unconcerned with its metaphysical justification, and frankly admitting that our present knowledge does not enable us demonstrably to relate it to the rest of the Cosmos. Let us glance at his method of treating Justice, at once the first and the last of moral problems :—

> I speak for those who do not believe in the existence of a Judge, unique, all-powerful and infallible, who, bending day and night over our thoughts, our sentiments, and our actions, maintains justice in this world, and completes it elsewhere. If there be no Judge, is there any justice in existence other than that organised by men, not only by their law and tribunals, but also in all social relations not submitted to positive judgment, and having, as a rule, no other sanction than that of opinion, the confidence or mistrust, the approbation or disapproval, of those who surround us? . . . When we have deceived or got the better of our neighbour, have we deceived and got the better of all the forces of justice? Is everything definitely settled, and have we nothing more to fear? Or does there exist a justice more serious and less liable to error, less visible but more profound, more universal and more powerful?

Man feels with irresistible conviction the existence of such a justice. But where does it dwell if the heavens be empty? It is not an idle question, for on the answer depends the whole of morality. Of three men, the first of whom bases his morality on the will of God, the second on a belief in some sort of physical justice, the third simply on his personal perception of justice, the third is the only one who interests the moralist. In him alone is morality really autonomous; and he alone will survive the other two. It is as certain as anything can be that the source of justice is nowhere in the physical universe around us. 'In the world in which we live there is no physical justice proceeding from moral causes, whether such justice be considered to present itself under the form of heredity, illness, or of atmospheric, geological, or any other phenomena imaginable.' Maeterlinck analyses a few of our more obvious illusions on the subject, and succeeds in showing, what no one who has seriously considered the question can doubt, that Nature only punishes breaches of physical law, with an entire disregard of the moral quality of such breaches. 'There is within us a spirit which weighs only intentions, there is without us a power which weighs only actions.' The 'spirit which weighs only intentions'; the source and only real sanction of morality can, however, act on what is without, modifying it to human ends, gradually substituting the hut for the cave, evolving the social pact out of the egotism of self-preservation, the family out of the vagrant impulses of the promiscuous savage. Thus a sort of physico-psychological justice is brought about which, corresponding within the sphere of phenomena subject to human action in a manner roughly tolerable to our desires, makes it possible for a moral creature to live without too much discomfort in a non-moral universe. 'Nature' frequently upsets this reign of human law by 'accidents,' and, more often perhaps, by a certain defect of comprehension, a certain slowness of adaptation to human needs, which is, at times, peculiarly exasperating. The idiotic volcano or the stupid storm will, at any moment, still for ever 'Shakespeare's brain or Lord Christ's heart.' Yet not altogether; and here Maeterlinck falls back on a conception which it is difficult not to call mystical: the conception of the dynamic unity of the universal human soul. Whether or not 'mute inglorious Miltons' lie in our churchyards, at least those who sing, sing to all of us and for ever. The peasant who passes has never heard of Plato; but had Plato not thought in such and such a way, his own thoughts would have been different. Wisdom, as in the old Jewish book, reaches from end to end, *fortiter et suaviter disponens omnia.* This fascinating doctrine lies outside experimental verification. It has a long history behind it; echoes of it come from the lecture halls of Alexandria and the banks of the Ganges; it seems implied in any adequate view of the 'interior life.' And there will always be those who will find in it the expression of their latent conviction; for it is one of the first, and not the least attractive, of the paths which open before humanity on its homing quest—if indeed it be so—back from the 'Many' to the 'One.' . . .

Apart, however, from such mysticism, Maeterlinck finds a stimulus in the analysis of the conditions of this man-made justice. Its reach is much wider, and its effect much deeper, than is commonly supposed. Here is a noble passage which cannot be laid too much to heart:—

> We willingly place under the heading, 'Injustice of the Universe,' a great number of injustices exclusively human and infinitely more frequent and more murderous than the tempest, illness and fire. I do not speak of war; it might be objected to me that it is attributed less to Nature than to the will of peoples or princes. But poverty, for instance, which we still place in the list of irresponsible evils like the plague or shipwreck, poverty with its crushing griefs and hereditary failures, how often is it not imputable to the injustice of our social state which is but the total of man's injustices? Why at the spectacle of an unmerited misery do we seek an heavenly judge or an impenetrable cause, as if it were the affair of a stroke of lightning? Do we forget that we find ourselves here in the best known and surest part of our own domain, and that it is we ourselves who organise misery and distribute it as arbitrarily, from a moral point of view, as the fire its ravages, or sickness its sufferings? Is it reasonable for us to wonder at the ocean for not taking account of the state of soul of its victim, when we, who have a soul, that is to say the organ *par excellence* of justice, pay no heed to the innocence of thousands of poor wretches who are our victims?

And to those who, with the 'complacent religiosity of the rich—that execrable sentiment,' would object that virtue and happiness are independent of material conditions, he replies:—

> If the child of our good neighbour be born blind, idiotic or deformed, we will go and seek, no matter where, even in the darkness of a religion we no longer practise, a God of some sort to interrogate his thought; but if the child be born poor, which usually lowers no less than the most serious infirmity by several degrees the destiny of a being, we shall not dream of asking a single question of the God who is everywhere where we are, since he is made of our will. Before desiring an ideal judge, it is necessary to purify our ideas. Before bewailing the indifference of Nature and seeking an equity which is not there, it were wise to attack, in our human regions, an iniquity which is there; and when it is there no longer, the part reserved for the injustices of chance will probably appear reduced by two-thirds. It will, in any case, be more diminished than if we had made the storm reasonable, the volcano perspicacious, the avalanche prewarned, heat and cold circumspect, sickness judicious, the sea intelligent and attentive to our virtues and secret intentions. There are, in fact, many more paupers than victims of shipwreck or material accidents, and many more maladies due to misery than to the caprices of our organism or the hostility of the elements.

Truly a comfortable doctrine, a sound and godly form of words. And woe to our ears if they are too delicate to hear them!

Of course this physico-psychological justice, besides being, after all, limited in its range, is evidently imperfect in its nature from a moral point of view. For though a moral intention is essential to it, that intention alone will not produce it. Power is required, and power in this case is knowledge. Such knowledge is within the reach of persons devoid of any morality. A despicable character might quite well discover the secret of what we call gravitation. And though the application of such knowledge to human needs would be materially moral, *i.e.* it would coincide with the wider uniformities of human well-being, it might, in the mind of its discoverer, be without any such quality. It would then pass the objective test of social morality; but it would lack that subjective sanction of conscious loyalty to ethical perception, without which there is for man no real morality whatever. The difficulty comes, not from the fact that there is no morality in the universe, for man is part of the universe and is moral; but from the fact that the power of the universe is not moral. The maxim that knowledge is power may serve well enough in the class-room; and power of a sort of course it is. But the power that is not knowledge, that recks nothing of its effects, envelops it as the ocean the drop of water. *Ces espaces infinies m'effraient!* And well they may; for their profoundest depths in which lie the destinies of all of us, are void of mind or conscience.

In his self-imposed task of the rationalisation and moralisation of his experience, Man is alone and, so far as he knows, unaided. On this point Maeterlinck does not hesitate. He eschews completely the dialectical *tours de force* of liberalising theologians. The Kingdom of Heaven, our natural inheritance, is solely within us; it exists only as an ideal, only in relation to human appreciation and discourse, that is, to our mind; Justice, Mercy, Beauty, Truth, are so many secretions of human consciousness, as silk is of the silk-worm.

In the antinomy between man's sense of justice and the indifference of the power which has brought him forth, our modern pessimists find the essential tragedy of humanity. 'A strange mystery it is,' said Mr. Bertrand Russell in a remarkable article published some years ago in the *Independent Review*,[1] 'that nature, omnipotent but blind, in the revolutions of her secular hurryings through the abyss of space, has brought forth, at last, a child, subject still to her power, but gifted with sight, with knowledge of good and evil, with the capacity of judging the works of his unthinking mother.'

But is not such pessimism based rather on mythology than fact; is it not, after all, but an after-effect of supernaturalism? For Nature is

[1] *Independent Review*, Dec. 1903, 'The Free Man's Worship.'

no mother from whom we spring; rather she comes to birth in our brain. It is only under the action of mind, and in relation thereto, that the term acquires either unity or value. Nature as a term of discourse, to which predicable values can be assigned, exists only in the same purely ideal manner as Truth, Beauty and Justice. The generalisations by means of which we organise what we call 'external,' are in our mind no less 'ideal' than those we employ in the construction of moral values; their locus is different, that is all. The Ideal is as natural as the Natural is ideal. It will nevertheless be said that, whether the universe be the child of our brain or we its product, makes no difference practically; equally the facts of experience are there, and we have to deal with them. It is amid those facts, the determination of which is beyond our conscious control, that our destiny is laid. Quite so; and it is from what is known of the human process, of the way in which man has dealt with these facts, in the past, that a sober and reasonable hope may be derived for the future. In one of his finest essays, *Les Rameaux d'Oliviers*, Maeterlinck states calmly his grounds for such hope. His argument there is, briefly, that such enormous difficulties, such terrible dangers, are now overcome, that we need not despair of the future. The law of man's progress has been the growth of his knowledge of his environment, which at first indeed appears hostile, but which, at the magic touch of human will and brain, shows itself more and more plastic. It is as if Nature were coming gradually to recognise her master, in proportion as that master enters by degrees into the kingdom of reason implicit in his consciousness. Man is, on the whole, wiser and better; civilisation, inadequate as its actual realisation may be, is, on the whole, more securely established than ever before on the planet; and the vistas of knowledge open more widely, more surely, more radiantly. If anything be needed to turn the balance of abstract consideration, we are justified in trusting to that indomitable courage, to that unflagging resolution of the human will, to realise by its creative power the ideals of the spirit which has brought us so far on our long pilgrimage.

I would venture to add a consideration which Maeterlinck nowhere explicitly mentions, although it seems to be implied in much that he says. By hypothesis Man is no supernatural being fallen from above into the universe. From the point of view of science, he is the result of the forces that at an earlier stage produced less complex manifestations of life. Does not this belief, instead of making for pessimism, as so many seem to think, rather furnish a strong ground for hope? If his origin were supernatural, then indeed Man might find himself at perpetual variance with his environment. But if he is himself the product of that environment, must not the equilibrium without which he could neither have appeared nor have maintained himself in existence come at length to express itself in the harmony of his consciousness? Maeterlinck is certainly one of those who contribute towards the grounds for thinking so, mainly by the exquisite single-mindedness with which he approaches the moral question, and which he inevitably communicates to a sympathetic reader. Not perhaps, since Pascal, has a European thinker vindicated so suggestively, so convincingly, the true dignity of the human intellect, the moral qualities inevitably inherent in the formation of opinion. And it is with those great words of Pascal, which so aptly resume the value of Maeterlinck as a moralist, that I will bring this essay to a close: 'All our dignity consists then in thought. It is from thought that we should take our point of departure, not from space or duration, which we can in nowise fill. Let us therefore labour to think correctly: that is the principle of morality.'

ANATOLE FRANCE

'THE longer I contemplate human life, the more I believe that we must give it, for witnesses and judges, Irony and Pity, even as the Egyptians evoked over their dead the goddesses Isis and Nephtis. Irony and Pity are two good counsellors. The one smiles and makes life amiable; the other weeps and makes it sacred. The irony which I invoke is not cruel. It mocks neither love nor beauty. It is gentle and kind. Its laugh calms anger; and it teaches us to smile at wicked men and fools whom, without it, we might have the weakness to hate.'

These are the words of a wise man and of a good man. They are, in addition, the profession of faith of perhaps the first living writer of French prose. M. Anatole France, the creator of Sylvestre Bonnard, of the Abbé Jérôme Coignard, of M. Bergeret, and of other charming companions of the hours snatched from those dreamlike futilities which make up what we call real life, is not only a writer of fiction. I do not like to say that he is greater than that, lest, in the event of these lines ever reaching the Master's eye, I should provoke a certain quiet smile, which, envisaged in imagination only, may well give the critic pause. At least I may be permitted to say that he is more than that. He is an historian of no common erudition ; he is a poet ; he is a philosopher.

The last qualification may be disputed. Since that birthday of philosophy on which our distant ancestor first observed that all serpents had more in common than of differentiation, philosophers have disagreed, not only on the proper way to conduct their business, but as to the precise nature of the business itself. Mr. Webster tells us that philosophy is 'the love of, including the search for, wisdom': thus revealing, in a phrase, the paradox at the core of every true philosopher's heart. For he loves what he has not found, what, doubtless, no man will ever find. He rises early and rests late, and diligently sweeps his house, like the woman in the parable ; but that precious penny still eludes his subtlest search. The wisest are those who, recognising this, find their account in so seemingly untoward a circumstance.

It can hardly be doubted that if, in an ill-advised moment, it were to occur to the high gods to repair their blunders by admitting man to the comprehension of their eternal counsels, the day that they did so would mark the beginning of the end of humanity. Thought would cease, and man would slowly begin with listless tread, to descend the angel-guarded ladder of flame which reaches from the earth of his origin to the heaven of his aspiration. And the place of his alighting would be no Bethel; it would be the primitive hole on the hillside, which, not so very long ago, he shared with rat and wolf. For curiosity is the mother of wisdom, last and most gratuitous, yet most essential of man's inventions; while life only maintains itself in virtue of a constant effort to surpass its achievement. Of these wisest philosophers is the subject of this essay.

M. France is of the line of the great sceptics, the salt of whose questionings has never been wanting to freshen the stream of human speculation. Far back that lineage stretches to legendary Pyrrho and fabled Kapila, and doubtless far beyond them again; for Doubt and Thought are the twin springs of the mind. The habit and aspect of the sceptic vary from age to age. He has, as a philosopher, no quarrel with the apparent values of experience; rather, with more than Protean ingenuity, he welcomes them all in turn. Let the banquet of life be as varied, as sumptuous, as delicate as possible; soon enough the cup must be turned down and the garland doffed.

Yon rising Moon that looks for us again—
How oft hereafter will she wax and wane;
How oft hereafter, rising, look for us—
Through this same garden and, for one, in vain!

Meanwhile that moon shines on Rose-in-hand's lips and eyes; and the scent of the night is on her hair and arms. Nor are these the only values of life. In an attic of a dormer-roofed, seventeenth-century Dutch house, sits a man still in the prime of life. He has left both his tables, the one strewed with manuscripts, the other with optical instruments, to watch a spider's duel. To a close observer, the brightness of his eye, the flush on his cheek surely indicate the mortal disease which in a year or two will cut him off. On the termination of the fight he returns to his desk, and writes the words: 'The free man thinks of nothing less than of death.' The calm peace of his expression, shining through the ravages of disease, shows that his heart is set on the love of the Eternal, the contemplation of which brings nothing but pure joy. Again. In a ravine of the Umbrian highlands kneels a man, clothed in ash-coloured sackcloth. His eyes red with weeping, are fixed on a roughly fashioned crucifix; his hands clasped in prayer, and his bare feet—O miracle of love!—are pierced and bedewed with blood. A wounded doe lies close, with broken leg deftly bound up by the

Saint's art, watching her master with liquid eye. She does not understand the meaning of his sighs and tears, but, being fain to comfort him, pokes, from time to time, a foolish tender muzzle among the folds of his robe. The Saint turns with a smile, and caresses his little friend; and the blood, which symbolises the ransom of mankind, stains her white-starred forehead, innocent alike of sin and redemption. Who shall estimate the rapture of that man? Also who, asks the sceptic, shall determine, without fear of gainsaying, whether the Persian reveller, Spinoza or St. Francis, be nearer to the truth of things?

Just as the sceptic looks with philosophic impartiality on the differing manifestations of life contained in the bosom of universal Nature, so also there is nothing in his system to prevent his adoption, for personal use, of such manifestations as may seem to him especially worthy.

According as heredity, circumstances, personal taste may dictate, he will be a voluptuary or an ascetic, a reactionary or a revolutionary, irreligious or devout. But in no case will he pay himself with words. If, for instance, he be devout, he will not attempt to sophisticate his mind or dim his soul with the fancied pros and cons of the case: he will frankly recognise his temperamental need of religion, and boldly rest his faith on those reasons of the heart of which the reason is ignorant, and which, however respectable as motives, are, in truth, as he well knows, no reasons at all. Of M. France it may be said that, though hardly to be called devout, he has certainly engaged himself 'on the side of the angels.'

Anatole François Thibault (the name 'France' is a pseudonym) was born in Paris in 1844. 'It seems to me impossible,' he says in his *Livre de Mon Ami*, the charming autobiography of his childhood, 'to have quite a commonplace mind if one has been brought up on the quays of Paris, in front of the Louvre and the Tuileries, near the Palais Mazarin, in front of the glorious Seine, flowing between the towers and turrets of old Paris.' His father, M. Noel Thibault, a well-known bibliophile, followed that most fascinating pursuit, the second-hand book trade. He was no ordinary bookseller, but employed his great knowledge in the collection of rare volumes. The talk of his father's friends provided a literary atmosphere for Anatole's childhood. Thus he learned the elements of the religion of books which, even in its fetichistic stage only, has consoled so many. His mother, towards whom he practised that *culte de la ma mère* which is so fine and general a note of the French character, was a simple and devout person, of warm heart and great good sense. It was her love, no doubt, that fostered that intensely human quality which was later to become so marked a characteristic of M. France's work at his best. Mme. Thibault would read saints' lives to the little Anatole with, on one occasion, somewhat surprising results. The episode is related in the *Livre de Mon Ami.*

My mother used often to read to me the Lives of the Saints, to which I listened with delight, and which filled my soul with surprise and love. I knew now how the men of the Lord managed to make their lives precious and full of merit; I knew the celestial fragrance diffused by the roses of martyrdom. But martyrdom was an extremity on which I did not decide. Nor did I dwell on the apostolate or on preaching which were hardly within my reach. I confined myself to austerities as being both easy and sure. In order to abandon myself to them without delay, I refused to eat my breakfast. My mother, who did not at all understand my new vocation, thought I was ill, and looked at me with an uneasiness which distressed me. But none the less I continued to fast. Then, recollecting St. Simon Stylites, who lived on the top of a column, I climbed on to the kitchen pump; but I could not live there, because Julia, the servant, promptly took me down. Having descended from my pump, I ardently rushed forward on the road of perfection and determined to imitate St. Nicholas of Patras, who distributed his riches to the poor. The window of my father's study overlooked the quay. I threw out of his window a dozen coppers which had been given me because they were new and shining; then I hurled out my marbles and tops and my big peg top with its eel-skin whip.

'This child is idiotic!' exclaimed my father, shutting the window. I experienced anger and shame at hearing myself judged in this way. But I reflected that my father, not being a saint like myself, would not share with me in the glory of the blessed; and this thought was a great consolation to me.

St. Theresa's childish dreams of martyrdom were shattered by contact with reality in the shape of a Philistine uncle. Anatole France's youthful aspirations after sanctity—he told his mother that he longed to write after his name *Ermite et Saint du Calendrier*, in emulation of the honorific suffixes which took so much room on his father's visiting cards—were dissolved by the even pressure, as one might say, by the force of inertia of the kindly irresponsive domestic atmosphere. Sanctity as a career was a failure; but the child was too thoroughly imbued with the national passion for 'la gloire' not to seek some other means of self-illustration. After all his unregenerate father, though heaven was closed to him, enjoyed much respect, and could write any number of 'soul-enhancing' epithets after his name. Perhaps his interests might furnish materials for a career. So the future Academician came to conceive his first literary project: that of writing a history of France in fifty volumes. At the moment of this resolution he was still of tender years, so tender, in fact, that he would weep when his nurse attended to such elementary details of his toilet as his nose. Moreover, he could not read. But, as he had already intuitively divined, material difficulties or even impossibilities do not operate in the same order of things as the idea. It may be well to add that these fifty volumes have never existed save *sub specie aeternitatis.* If space permitted, I could linger much longer over this charming book, written in the perfection of M. France's style, in the maturity of his genius; it was published in 1885. It is an unusually happy specimen of the genre Confessions. The fresh ingenuousness of its manner is rare enough in autobiography.

As he grew older, his father sent him to the well-known Collége Stanislaus. Here that taste for Greek and Roman antiquity, which has through life meant so much to him, declared itself unmistakably. He was fascinated by Sophocles and Virgil. Not altogether, however, in a way agreeable to his professors. The boy was a dreamer, and loved to wander down those bypaths of scholarship which do not lead to success in examinations. He tells us that his 'Latin prose contained solecisms.' Another cause of his unpopularity with his teachers was his strongly marked inclination to elude the religious discipline which was so accentuated a feature of Mgr. Dupanloup's educational system.

As he said at Tréguier, of Renan, his mind realised very quickly the difficulties of belief. Or rather, perhaps, his imaginative outlook was filled up and contented by the great figures of classical antiquity in a way which left no void for religion to fill. He says, to quote once more from the *Livre de Mon Ami*:—

> I saw Thetis, rising like a white cloud over the sea. I saw Nausicaa and her companions, and the palm-tree of Delos, and the sky and the earth, and the ocean, and Andromache smiling through her tears. . . . I understood. I felt. It was impossible for me for six months to put down the *Odyssey*.

The ancient gods had forestalled their successor; Anatole France as a child was *anima naturaliter pagana.*

M. France commenced author with a small volume of verse called *Vers Dorés*, under the ægis of Leconte de Lisle. But the orthodoxy of Parnassus soon became too strait for him; and the great man does not seem to have taken in good part the heresies and, at last, the complete defection of his brilliant but too individualist disciple. Poetry, however, of which he has always remained an ardent lover and penetrating critic, was not to him a really authentic means of self-expression. He had the faculty of writing verse, as most great literary artists have; but prose was the medium most fitted for his essentially meditative and discursive nature. He soon produced his *Thaïs*, a veritable poem in prose, in which the luxurious tones of Byzantine decadence were artfully married with the bleak ascetic values of the Egyptian desert. M. France has always had a weakness for monachism, and has frequently returned to the subject.

The work which first really called on him the attention of the public was *Le Crime de Sylvestre Bonnard*, published in 1881, which was crowned by the Academy. In this delightful book, France recreated the type of the old *savant* whose innocent egotism is qualified by a more than average dose of human kindness. The reader will not expect to be taken through a *catalogue raisonné* of M. France's work. One may say briefly, that he has written a great deal, and hardly anything except, perhaps, if the criticism may be ventured, *Le Lys Rouge* and the *Histoire Comique*, that is without the peculiar and intimate charm that has come to be associated with his name.

It is in *La Rôtisserie de la Reine Pédauque* and its sequel, *Les Opinions de M. Jérôme Coignard*, that he has succeeded in expressing himself supremely. In these books his fantasy and (an enemy would say) his sophistry are suffused with so rich a glow of kindly humanity as to be quite irresistible. We may disapprove of the Abbé Coignard: it is our right as law-abiding citizens and respectable churchmen to do so; but it is impossible even to think of him without secret joy. Poor M. Jérôme! so great and so little, so noble and so vile, who forgets his cassock in the tavern, and his priesthood in the arms of the 'femme de chambre de Madame la Baillive'; who discourses of morals with the eloquence of Seneca, yet cheats at cards and pilfers jewels; who combines the most daring flights of speculation with the simplicity of true Christian faith; and who, after a vagabond existence among wenches and pot-boys, eked out, according to circumstances, by deciphering Egyptian manuscripts or writing love-letters for maid-servants, finally dies a holy and edifying death from the effects of a wound received in the course of a disreputable adventure—what are we to say of him, and why do we love him? The reason of our love is not far to seek. And we may turn for it to a doctor of the Abbé Coignard's communion. In the *Dream of Gerontius*, Cardinal Newman sums up the balance sheet of a man as:—

> Majesty dwarfed to baseness, poisonous flower running to seed;
> Who never art so near to crime and shame
> As when thou hast achieved some deed of name.

We love M. Jérôme Coignard because he is a living, sensible epitome of humanity, of our own hearts. Thus and thus are we, though it may not suit us to admit the fact. And, oddly enough, in spite of this invincible disinclination, the vicarious unveiling of our own hearts gives us a pleasure of a most delightful quality, such epicures in moral sensation have we become. It gives us the illusion of the confession we shall never make, of the sincerity we shall never achieve. And the illusion also of that peace of heart, which, as theologians assure us, is the accompaniment and reward of true contrition. So we have ample motives for loving M. Jérôme Coignard. This great and good man, at once philosopher and hedge priest, a splendid toper and an accomplished scholar, is first introduced to us in the roasting shop of Léonard Ménétrier, who plies his laudable trade in the Rue St. Jacques, at the sign of *La Reine Pédauque.* Here the Abbé finds his daily cover laid in return for the instructions which he gives the roaster's son Jacques, commonly called Tournebroche, in virtue of the office which he shares with the dog Miraut. This Jacques becomes his master's devoted disciple and biographer. We will not follow them through their adventures, which include the frequentation of a charming and crazy hermetic philosopher (an admirably reconstructed eighteenth-century type), some incidental fighting, and more than one episode of the kind that, in France, legitimately adds to the gaiety of life, and, in England, is never mentioned. Let us, rather, briefly dwell on the ideas conveyed by these delightful books. They represent, with the conversations of M. Bergeret in the four volumes of the *Histoire Contemporaine*, the ripest moods of M. France's philosophy, a philosophy which, due allowance being made for temperamental variations—the inevitable sanction of which is one of its principal charms—is held, in substance, by many of the best minds in Europe to-day.

I have already indicated the school of thought to which M. France belongs. He is of the great school of Elis, the school of Pyrrho. With the *nuance*, however, of his time. He has expressly told us, in his answer to M. Brunetière, who had attacked him as a mere subjectivist, self-dispensed from the arduous labour of exact knowledge, that he believes in 'the relativity of things and the succession of phenomena': that is in science. M. France believes then in science; but let not dogmatists of any kind, even those who frequent the Royal Institution, presume to hail him as a fellow. 'What,' asks the Abbé Coignard, 'is the knowledge of Nature but the fantasy of our senses?' This is discouraging; and it seems as if the saintly immobility, the blessed ataraxy of the fakir, would be the practical translation of such an attitude. On the contrary, no man is more interested in life than he. No detail of humanity's long pilgrimage escapes his affectionate curiosity. His faithful love of men and their doings is, rather than the mere abstract passion of erudition, at the bottom of his ceaseless interest in history. The fact is that the teachings of Pyrrho are at once reinforced in his mind, and qualified by those of another Greek philosopher, the divine Epicurus.

Walter Savage Landor used to say that we should walk through life with Epicurus on the one hand and Epictetus on the other. In a similar vein M. France says that the former philosopher and St. Francis of Assisi are the two best friends—and mutual correctives—that humanity has found on its path through the world. The Stoic rigour is alien to his temperate and kindly wisdom: 'Il ne faut pas exagérer le mal que l'on fait.' Rather would he extol the golden moderation of the garden philosopher, and dwell on the Preacher's advice not to be wise overmuch. The temper of that colony perched on 'a certain breezy tableland projecting from the African coast,' of which Mr. Pater has written so delightfully, is his. A true Cyrenaic, Horace's summing up of the philosophy of the founder of Cyrene may be justly applied to him: *omnis Aristippum decuit color et status et res.*

Indeed, Aristippus is nearer to him than Pyrrho. The latter had thrown the universal doubt that lies coiled at the root of knowledge—'the little dead red worm therein'—into a blank abstract interrogative; but he, apparently, did not realise that life and speculation are two things, that, even though both we ourselves and the appearances that dance over our sensorium, are from the point of view of speculative analysis, but vain shadows together, that fact does not make them or us any less interesting, does not even tend to lower or qualify in any way their human value. For it is evident that that value springs wholly from the undeniable experience of relation; what exactly is related to what is irrelevant. At least it is charitable to suppose that, when Pyrrho passed his master Aristarchus wailing for help in a ditch, on the ground that his unfortunate plight stood in need of metaphysical proof, he mixed up two things. And it is certainly impossible to imagine that M. France would have left Renan, his one master among moderns, in a ditch for such reasons.

It is characteristic of M. France's detachment from popular, or indeed any kind of polemics, that, while he himself remains scrupulously, and it would seem unregretfully un-Christian, his most important philosophical protagonist should be a Catholic priest. No doubt he has expressed his personal attitude more fully in his Bergeret of the *Histoire Contemporaine.* But M. Bergeret is by no means so convincing or so attractive as M. Coignard. Dare one say it? He is at times distinctly tedious. Whether it is that he suffers unduly from his sordid domestic surroundings, or from the stifling atmosphere of his gossiping little university, or from what strikes a foreign observer as the abject provincialism of contemporary French public life, one certainly grows weary of him. Not so of M. Coignard. To him M. France has dispensed all his inimitable charm; he has lavished on him the finest resources of his art. That he should have done so is, as I have said, characteristic of his detachment from popular causes; it also surely indicates the exquisite fairness, the crystalline probity of his mind. Not thus are philosophers wont to treat philosophers who have the misfortune to differ from them. Schopenhauer—no doubt the case was exceptional—called Hegel by name and in print an 'intellectual Caliban' and a 'charlatan.' But to return to our Abbé!

I cannot do better than make some quotations from M. France's own analysis of his hero:—

I am not afraid to affirm that M. l'Abbé Coignard, philosopher and Christian, united in an incomparable combination the Epicureanism that preserves us from pain and the holy simplicity that leads us to joy. It is remarkable that, not only did he accept the idea of God as it was provided for him by the Catholic faith, but also that he endeavoured to maintain it by arguments of a rational order. He never imitated the practical ability of professional Deists who make, for their own use, a God, at once moral, philanthropic, and modest (*pudique*), with whom they enjoy the satisfaction of a perfect understanding. The close relations which they establish with him procure for their writings a great deal of authority, and for their persons much consideration from the public. And this governmental God, moderate, solemn, free from all fanaticism, and who knows the world (*qui a du monde*), recommends them in assemblies, drawing-rooms, and academies. M. l'Abbé Coignard did not fashion to himself so profitable an Eternal. But, reflecting that it is impossible to conceive of the universe, except under the categories of the intelligence, and that the Cosmos must be held to be intelligible, even in view of the demonstration of its absurdity, he referred its cause to an intelligence which he called God, leaving to this term its infinite vagueness, while for the rest he went to theology, which, as we know, treats of the unknowable with a minute exactitude. This reserve which marks the limits of his intelligence was a happy one if, as I think, it removed from him the temptation to nibble at some appetising system of philosophy, and saved him from pushing his nose into one of those mouse-traps in which the emancipated spirits hasten to get caught. At his ease in the great old rat-hole, he found more than one issue through which to discover the world and observe nature. I do not share his religious beliefs, and I think that they deceived him, as they have deceived for their happiness and misery so many generations of men. But it would seem that the ancient errors are less annoying than the modern ones, and that, since we must be deceived, the better part for us is to cling to the illusions which have lost their roughness.

So much for the Abbé Coignard's metaphysic and theology. His attitude towards the latter was that of no less a thinker than Descartes, who placed his theology under the ægis of Père Mersenne. Let us now hear M. France on his ethic.

Never did human spirit show itself at once so bold and so pacific, or steep its disdain in greater sweetness. His ethic united the liberty of the cynical philosophers with the candour of the first friars of the holy Portiuncula. He despised men with tenderness; he tried to teach them that the only side on which they had a little grandeur being a capacity for pain, the one useful and beautiful quality for them was pity; that able only to desire and suffer, they should make to themselves indulgent and voluptuous virtues. He thus came to consider pride the only source of the greatest evils, and the only vice contrary to nature. It would seem indeed that men make themselves miserable by the exaggerated feeling which they have for themselves and their kind, and that, if they had a humbler and truer idea of human nature, they would be gentler to each other and themselves. It was his benevolence which urged him to humiliate his fellows in their sentiments, their knowledge, their philosophy, and their institutions. He had it at heart to show them that their imbecile nature has neither imagined nor constructed anything worthy of a very energetic attack or defence, and that, if they knew the fragility and simplicity of their greatest works, such as their laws and their empires, they would fight for them only in play and for fun, like children who build sand castles on the beach. Moreover, one should not be either astonished or scandalised at the fact that he abased all the ideas by which man exalts his glory and honour at the expense of his repose. The majesty of the law did not impose on his clear-sighted soul; and he regretted that poor wretches should be subjected to so many obligations of which, in most cases, one can discover neither the origin nor the meaning. All principles seemed to him equally contestable. He had come to believe that citizens only condemned so many of their kind to infamy in order to enjoy by contrast the joys of public respect. This view made him prefer bad company to good, after the example of Him who lived among publicans and prostitutes. He preserved there purity of heart, the gift of sympathy, and the treasures of mercy.

M. Coignard's philosophy showed to special advantage in his criticism of social justice, militarism, magistrates, police, and political institutions generally. Not one did his genial and mordant analysis leave standing. Yet he was no revolutionary. He was, as he said, like the old woman of Syracuse, who prayed for the preservation of the existing tyrant—the worst, she observed, that there had ever been—on the ground that a still worse one would surely succeed him. He seems to have believed in what human improvement he thought possible, on the ground of an ingenious application to moral and social matters of the law of 'actual causes.' Sir Charles Lyell, as is known, maintained, some fifty years ago, that the various changes that have come about in the earth's surface during the course of the ages were not due, as was then commonly supposed, to sudden cataclysms, but to the gradual operation of slow and imperceptible causes, which to this day continue their silent invisible task of transforming the crust of the planet. M. Coignard seems to have applied the analogy of Lyell's theory to the phenomena of social growth and development. For instance, he hated war, partly on moral grounds, and partly, no doubt, because, as Fontenelle said, it interrupted conversation. He looked forward to its disappearance, not as the result of any conscious effort of humanity, such as the forcible establishment of courts of arbitration and the like, but rather as the inevitable consequence of a perfect balance of power, to be brought about at last by the equalisation of the armaments of rival states. The evil would thus kill itself. Similarly, the absurdities of legal justice would at length reach such a point as gradually to melt away of themselves before the irony of a human being, the son of our loins, rather more clear-sighted than his parents, but not in any way essentially differing from them. So, then, the Abbé Coignard believed in justice, and, so far, was no sceptic? Yes, he believed in justice, and in 'whatsoever things are of good report'; but he did not think that the home of these things was among men. Justice was to him the vanishing point of the perspective of human society, the ideal existence of which is necessarily implied in all human aspiration, while its achievement, as a fact, is as necessarily denied to all human effort.

We may note here a profound difference between the Abbé Coignard's doctrine and that of the Revolution. That great movement in human affairs was based on the belief in the natural justice of Man. Condorcet is as clear on this point as Jean-Jacques. The Abbé Coignard would have said that man, being naturally unjust, tends obscurely and intermittently to improve himself in the direction of justice, but that unjust he is by nature and unjust by nature he always will remain. He held no illusions about humanity. Had he been able, with prophetic mind, to gauge the great biological generalisation which has in modern times so profoundly modified all our thoughts concerning man and his destiny, there is little doubt that he would have sided with Darwin against Rousseau. His principal objection to the philosophy of the latter would have been that it assumed an unscientific difference of kind between the gorilla and its human descendant. So he may, in a sense, be considered as the precursor of the modern *rétrograde éclairé*. There is, at least, little doubt that were he among us to-day, the party represented by that superior person would on the whole have his approval. I do not, of course, mean that all its contemporary manifestations, particularly in France, would have his support. Rather his sense of irony, not to mention his Christian charity, would detach him from not a few of its methods. But, on the whole, the attitude would have his approval.

M. Bergeret in the *Histoire Contemporaine* is the other most important incarnation of M. France's thought. Here we have another type of sceptic. The Abbé Coignard had not much faith in men, but he had plenty of faith in God: and his ideal beliefs, far from dimming his vision of actuality, served, on the contrary, to make it keener. He whose trust was in the Eternal could afford to recognise to the full the absurdity of passing events. His religious faith kept his heart sound and his moral nature sweet and true to the essential norms of human instinct. He was pure in heart because he saw God. M. Bergeret did not see God, and in human life saw little else than a wilful mass of indecent absurdity. And in consequence M. Bergeret was unhappy. He did not merely suffer from passing low spirits. He was permanently, radically, essentially unhappy. Nevertheless in spite of his unhappiness, he is, in a sense, a more mature expression of his Creator's philosophy than the Abbé Coignard.

That Anatole France is an individualist of the finest water is sufficiently evident from everything he has ever said or written. It is his nature to form his own opinions in his own way and solely for his own gratification. The vitality of his contribution is due to the intensity with which it expresses now this, now that aspect of his extraordinarily versatile personality. His method of criticism displayed more clearly in the four volumes of his *Vie Littéraire* than in his professedly imaginative work, is a significant self-revelation. It consists in a certain subtle and sympathetic penetration, which almost reaches the point of self-identification with his subject. It is in this way that he produces his illusion of objectivity. Thus, whether he is writing of Asiatic religions, contemporary literature, science or philosophy, his subject seems to be spontaneously yielding up its inmost secret to the compelling courtesy of his investigation as a flower yields its perfume to the caresses of the sun. For he treats all ideas with the uniform and exquisite politeness of the sceptic. Indeed his scepticism is an important part of his success as a critic. It is after all not until an idea has ceased to be an ideal that it becomes a fruitful subject for criticism.

Anatole France evidently represents a more developed, a more philosophical scepticism than any other writer noticed in these studies. His position is roughly that our only knowledge is science, and that that only knowledge besides bearing solely on the relations of things, not on their nature, and, therefore, in no way dispelling our essential ignorance of them, is at any given point, owing to the progressive method by which we acquire it, more wrong than right. For the science of to-day so transforms that of yesterday as to make it false, and there will always be to-morrow to be counted with. Nevertheless the method of science, *i.e.* the application of the category of causation to the connections of phenomena, while telling us nothing whatever about their intimate nature or even their real existence, which it assumes and leaves for ever totally unexplained and unproved, is, subjectively speaking, the legitimate development of the instinct of knowledge. It is in scientific terms the 'law' of that instinct, which merely means that that is the way in which that instinct behaves when it reaches maturity. Behind this fact of our nature—for it is a psychological fact that so and not otherwise does our mind work—it is impossible to go. It is equally impossible to discuss its validity as a philosophical principle, for, in order to do so, we have to assume it: it is therefore but waste of breath either to attribute or deny to it metaphysical cogency. This fully developed scepticism is a very different matter from the scepticism of the eighteenth century. That movement emancipated the human mind from theology; the sceptic of to-day is emancipated from the superstition of reason. The first emancipation leaves the mind anxious and ill at ease, at times a ready prey, on the rebound, for some new fashion of credulity, and if the intellectual character is too strongly knit to find a fancied peace in such a solution, suffering, in proportion to the emotional depth of a man's nature, must ensue. Mérimée is a case in point. But when error is torn up by the roots, when the mind is emancipated from the illusion of reason no less than from that of theology, man begins at last to live. He acquiesces in the limitations of his cerebral convolutions, he is resigned to his lot. Nay, he comes to love it with all its defects, with all its drawbacks. 'Ma petitesse m'est chère!' cries M. France, and Nietzsche's 'Amor Fati' is nothing but a more grandiloquent phrase for the same feeling. Accepting his destiny in no grudging spirit, doing, that is cheerfully and with full *connaissance de cause* what in any case he must do, the sceptic turns himself to the loving cultivation of human nature. And he finds his sufficient reward. For now a miracle happens. The sword of his intelligence, which snapped like a silvered lathe when employed on immensities and incomprehensibilities, becomes, when turned to its true uses, a sure and tempered weapon in his hand. Art and science and the cautious betterment of human lot within the limits of human nature, are the appropriate objects on which his 'Practical Reason' exercises itself.

There are those who see in the fact that M. France has devoted himself of late years to the furtherance of social justice a backsliding from his intellectual ideals. The criticism is, I think, a petty one. It is indeed legitimate to question the wisdom of his methods. We may reasonably doubt that the socialistic tendencies which he encourages will, if triumphant, produce what he hopes for, but that it is irrational for a sceptic to endeavour to make himself and his fellow-creatures more comfortable on this peculiar planet is itself the most irrational of propositions. A great living philosopher tells us, that even if we are all going to Hell next week it is worth while, in the interval, to read Robert Browning in preference to Robert Montgomery. Equally, whatever be the ultimate destiny of humanity, even if the phrase have, in strict thought, no meaning, it is important that existing humanity should be as happy and successful as the nature of things permits.

The belief in the universal flux of things, in the absence of any ascertainable moral or intellectual order in the world, has represented the conviction of some of the serenest and finest of human intelligences. It was the mental attitude of an Epicurus, a Democritus, a Montaigne, a Gassendi. M. France has put it before us once more with unrivalled clearness and beauty of expression, and with a modernity of touch that makes it move in our minds as an actual form of our own experience. The sheet lightning of his quiet irony illuminates it; and the glow of his pity suffuses it with an irresistibly attractive humanity. To have rendered thus perfectly, with so fine and conscientious an art, his personal vision of life, gives him his supreme claim on our admiration, on our intelligent sympathy. The commerce of wisdom, we are told by the Preacher, is pleasant. Those who doubt it cannot do better than turn to the works of Anatole France.

EPILOGUE

NOTES ON THE PHILOSOPHY OF DISILLUSION[1]

THE faith in reason of the philosophers of the eighteenth century, however noble and socially beneficial an attitude, was not, and could not be, the permanent resting-place of the human mind. Montesquieu, Voltaire, and Diderot, to take three different types of eighteenth-century thinkers, were all agreed, in spite of their personal differences, on the point that the unfettered use of reason was all that was needed to place man in possession of truth and happiness. Their position involved two important *a priori* principles, emphatically articles of faith, not of reason; and neither more nor less articles of faith than the fundamental tenets of the

[1] It need hardly be said that these 'Notes' are not intended as a formal exposition of the Philosophy of Disillusion. They are merely meant to suggest and illustrate certain positions which are more widely held to-day than those who do not hold them may think. Those who wish to study the subject in systematic detail cannot do better than refer to the works of M. Jules de Gaultier and of M. Remy de Gourmont, published by the Société du Mercure de France, Paris.

Church. They assumed, prior to all investigation, the completely rational nature of reality, and the essential goodness of all men. The disillusion of these men was the result of the conquest of one faith by another. That is to say, it was not, properly speaking, a fundamental disillusion. Faith in man took the place of faith in God, Paradise became the ultimate state of society to which reason was tending, Providence, when science came to eke out their conceptions, became evolution, God became immanent in and indistinguishable from man; and, in the case of the true devotees of humanity, the religious symphony was merely transferred into another key.

There was thus a symbolic fitness in the worship of the Goddess of Reason on the dismantled altar of Notre Dame. The Altar, the principle of religion, remained, it was only the object of worship that was changed. The well-meaning people who organised that remarkable function, like their earliest predecessors in the attempt to destroy Christianity, knew not what they did. Had they pushed their philosophical analysis so far as to criticise their new deity, they would have realised that it was no more unreasonable to worship the Sacred Host of Christian tradition, than an unusually stout courtesan. That analysis indeed, had they but known it, was already, in its essentials, complete. The *Critique of Pure Reason* had appeared twelve years before the apotheosis of Mlle. Candeille.

The work of Kant was of the most revolutionary description. In the course of his Transcendental Dialectic, he refutes the ontological proof of the existence of God, the argument of St. Anselm, Descartes and Leibnitz. He equally shows the inanity of the other two traditional arguments, the physico-theological and the cosmological, which had been the mainstay of the philosophy of the Catholic Schools. On the other hand, the antitheses in the second and third Antinomies show the impossibility of the existence of a simple substance, and consequently of the soul, in the theological sense of the term, and destroy the possibility of human liberty in an ordered universe. The main theses of the philosophers of the French enlightenment were thus pricked. Most of them, indeed, were Deists, and even the Atheists required a moral Absolute. Kant's intellect, however, was one thing, and his temperament another. The evangelical Christian could not endure the conclusions of the philosopher, and the *Critique of Practical Reason* laboured to restore the spiritualist positions of which the first Critique had made short work. Resuming the conclusions of the first Critique in the proposition that God, Freedom and Immortality were indemonstrable, and therefore unknowable to Pure Reason, Kant here insists on their 'practical' truth, which, when analysed, comes to mean that it is wise for creatures situated as we are to believe them to be true.

At the side of the great metaphysical poems of Fichte, Hegel, Lötze and other minor post-Kantian thinkers, the philosophy of disillusion has pursued its course through the nineteenth century from the *Critique of Pure Reason* through Schopenhauer to Nietzsche. It has consisted in the development of Kant's idealism into a purely subjective phenomenalism. To put its main conclusion less technically, it has shown, not from abstract considerations but by means of an analysis of the act of knowledge as it occurs in our experience, that thought cannot transcend the strictly relative co-ordination of experience. The Absolute Realities, which form the theme of the various dogmatic systems which derive directly or indirectly from Platonism, it has shown (incompletely in the *Critique of Pure Reason*; with completeness in Schopenhauer's *Fourfold Root of the Principle of Sufficient Reason*) to be nothing but the lenses through which the faculty of knowledge represents to itself the notion of external existence. The important discovery of Schopenhauer was not the oriental myth of the self-realising and the self-annihilating Will of the World, but his simple and irrefutable statement that the act of knowledge betrayed on analysis its own relativity, consisting, as it necessarily did, of the representation of an object for a subject, thus implying an essential dualism. From this impregnable position it was easy to show that the doctrine of an absolute knowledge identified in its inmost nature with absolute being involved a meaningless proposition. The roots of Theism, as a philosophical explanation of the world, were cut away. M. Jules de Gaultier, who represents better than any contemporary the Philosophy of Disillusion to-day, has pointed out in his excellent book, *De Kant à Nietzsche*, that Kant, while preparing the way for Schopenhauer's theological Nihilism, had, even in the first Critique, endeavoured to cover his own traces. 'What Kant is careful not to say,' observes M. de Gaultier, 'no matter how strong the evidence which constrains him to say it, is that the idea of a First Cause, taken as a transcendental concept, is, in the highest degree, one of those concepts which are formed in contradiction to the laws of reason, and which have only to be formulated to be disavowed. Reason furnishes us with the principle of causality, with which to arrange the phenomenal world: everything which exists, exists in virtue of a cause. A cause then being a thing which exists, the right deduction, in order to manifest the principle in its blinding light, is that every cause has a cause. That is the principle of reason which must not be transgressed, and which the idea of a First Cause, a cause without a cause, directly violates.' And M. de Gaultier goes on to observe, with a lucidity which many philosophers might envy: 'When the reason seeks an explanation of the universe, it goes without saying that that explanation must be intelligible to the reason. The intelligence is in a state of ignorance before the mystery, the question of the reason demands a reply which shall dissipate that ignorance. Now to attempt to dissipate that ignorance by the application of the principle of causality in its legitimate form to the Whole of phenomena, considered as the effect of a cause situated outside that Whole, is, on the one hand, a kind of anthropomorphism, but, above all, it explains nothing, because the form of the principle of causality will forthwith oblige the mind to seek for the cause of that cause outside the world, remounting indefinitely in the void from cause to cause. If, in order to obviate this inconvenience, theology forms the concept of a First Cause, no more real explanation is given, for the addition of a word cannot change the nature of reason, and make intelligible what was unintelligible before: mystery is not explained by the incomprehensible. . . . To explain the existence of the universe by means of this concept is to propose to the reason to admit that two plus two equals five, and to insinuate that at the price of that concession hitherto insoluble problems can be solved.' M. de Gaultier relates this divergent branching of Kant's intellect and temperament to what he considers to be the general law of philosophical development, and which is, at least, a more than ingenious hypothesis. It is this. The Vital Instinct and the Instinct of Knowledge, far from being the allies that popular educationalists proclaim them to be, are at secret war with each other. The Vital Instinct expresses itself at the origin of one of those groups of human beings that we call a race, in a collection of moral, physical and mental attitudes, that have nothing to do with the question of truth, but that represent more or less successfully the conditions of its durability and power to the extent to which the race is conscious of them at that moment. These prescriptions are the work of a law-giving priesthood, and are codified in religious forms, that is, in taboos. It seems an acquired fact that they are always represented as the teaching of revelation, never as the result of observation or knowledge. In process of time, the Instinct of Knowledge awakes in some sceptic, whose vitality is declining, and if he cannot be suppressed, he has to be answered. And now occurs a curious inversion of rôles. The Vital Instinct disguises itself as the Instinct of Knowledge, and if unable to save the old myth, promptly invents a new one to take its place. In an advanced community, where an appeal to reason is implied in all propositions, the myth is philosophical rather than crudely naturalistic in construction. But it is no less a myth, that is, a transposition into such terms of reality, as the community is prepared imaginatively to accept, of the vital needs of the moment. M. de Gaultier illustrates this thesis by an analysis of the dogma of Monotheism. The dogma consists of belief in a God, external to the world, who is its creator, revealing, either miraculously, by infringing the determinism elsewhere observable, or naturally, by inspiration in human consciousness, a moral law, *i.e.* a good to practise and an evil to avoid. It involves also the belief in man's free will, by means of which he is capable of observing or disobeying the law, thus incurring merit or demerit, and deserving punishment or reward. Monotheism springs, historically speaking, from two distinct roots, Judaism and the philosophy of Plato. In its purely religious form, that of direct revelation, it represents the categorical imperative of the Vital Instinct, asserting itself in a manner beyond any question of rational proof. *It is so because life is so, not because we think it to be so.* It is otherwise with Monotheism considered as a philosophical explanation of the world. In this case proof is required, and it is here that M. de Gaultier detects the deforming effect of the Vital Instinct on the mechanism of the intellect.

The enigma of knowledge presents itself under a triple aspect to Plato. There is first the scientific question, how do we know external objects? Then there are the two other categories of objects, those of the moral and those of the metaphysical world, already created in a rudimentary fashion by the Vital Instinct, which demands that the philosopher should complete the work begun. These objects, being the creation of the mind, are, of course, very easy to handle. They are not under the control of space or time; never appearing in the phenomenal world, which cannot exist except in space and time, they can easily brave any possible refutation from experience. It is easy to believe them to be of the same nature as the intelligence which conceives them; then, all that is necessary is once for all to declare them endowed with existence, outside as well as within the mind. The ruse here, consists in the fact that the mind being unable to explain the fact of knowledge by the fact of existence, quietly reverses the terms of the problem, and attributes to knowledge the power to create being. It is exactly the same process, in the intellectual sphere, as that of primitive man constructing his idols, and then persuading himself that he owes to them his own existence.

The whole of this process, when it is dealing with the objects of the moral or metaphysical world, is, as has been said, beyond the possibility of experimental verification or refutation. The vagueness of content of these objects, compared to the definiteness of the objects of the external world, is also a further protection to the vicious construction of the process. Let us observe it at work on the fundamental problem of knowledge; how do we know of the existence of external objects in the phenomenal world?

The knowledge of an object, says the Platonic Socrates, supposes that a definition can be given of it, and to define is to classify and limit under the category of a general idea. But this general idea, which confers on the object knowable existence, does not itself belong to the object. Nor can it be derived from the senses which give us, at the most, very incomplete information about objects. Where will Plato find the *locus* of these ideas, the necessary intermediaries of our knowledge? Not in human reason, for they are, he says, its objects, being independent of human reason, in the same way as external objects are independent of the senses. It is in the Divine Reason, of which they are the attributes, that these ideas, the eternal types of the particular objects, perceived by the senses, have their real and substantial existence. This is the doctrine of the Platonic Ideas, and if the greatness of philosophic doctrines is to be measured by their influence and duration, it is undoubtedly one of the greatest. It is still, after twenty-four centuries, the ill-disguised backbone of all absolute metaphysic, and the substance of all theology, which claims, in any sense, to incorporate reason.

From the point of view of logic, it is, however, singularly vulnerable. I know the dog of Alcibiades by means of the idea of dog, I proceed in abstraction to the idea of a mammal, from that to the idea of an animal in general, from that to the idea of existence in general. But does on that account existence in general exist? Is there outside my mind an object which can be called existence in general? Evidently not. Existence abstracted from any particular existence, is nothing but a category of the mind indispensable to the representation of external objects, all of which are said to exist, because the act of knowledge necessarily groups them under that category in itself nothing but a pure mental form.

This *quiproquo*, by means of which thought *adds*

to its legitimate function of regulating reality the pretension to create it, is, as has been said, the source of all religious philosophy, it is also at the bottom of all philosophy that implies the recognition of any other than a purely phenomenal value in phenomena. All schemes of 'progress' that represent experience as moving by its own nature towards the realisation of an intellectual or a moral absolute, depend upon it. Even Pragmatism, the fashion of the moment, in spite of its jaunty disclaimer of metaphysic, is, at least, its illegitimate descendant.

Philosophy, like the kingdom of Heaven, has rarely been sought for its own sake alone, and the consequences of philosophical disillusion extend further than the purely intellectual domain. I have said that to refuse to admit the creation of reality by thought excludes the belief in the existence of absolute values in experience. Morality, in the sense that it has commonly been understood during the reign of the Platonic Ideas, must go. Kant's miraculous Categorical Imperative is an empty phrase, *bombinans in vacuo*, not so much false as entirely meaningless. Conduct appeals primarily to utility, secondarily to taste, virtue recovers its etymological meaning and becomes again the *virtus* of the Romans. We appreciate human beings, like wines, by their qualities. If their behaviour is hostile to a few obviously recognised utilities we call them criminals, and suppress or shut them up if we can. At a further stage of discrimination, if we find them unattractive, we avoid them—if we are wise. There is no mystery about this. Here, if anywhere, we are *chez nous*. It is simply a question of affinities and reactions; as it were, a chemical problem. At identical stages of culture, ethical prepossession, *i.e.* taste in conduct, tends appreciably to repeat itself unchanged in different individuals, which agreement constitutes a social sanction to the taste of the group. But that agreement guarantees merely a social sanction. The fact that most people like dry champagne does not constitute that taste an absolute value. There is no difference of kind between moral qualities and good manners.

There is no doubt that such conclusions as these are wellnigh intolerable to many people. In fact, roughly speaking, it is only those in whom the instinct of knowledge has corroded their vitality who can endure them complacently. Such as they find their greatest joy in the gratification of their intellect, and the justification of the world to them consists solely in its spectacular value. The Vital Instinct may be trusted to keep them in a permanent minority, for too many of them would bring humanity to an end. They will not, however, disappear—except, indeed, possibly by violence! For the work of the analysis of the faculty of knowledge has been done, and those, whose minds are so constructed as to be able to appreciate the process will not be able to escape its conclusions. Nor are they really so dangerous to the interests of the Vital Instinct as some of its champions may think. 'On peut dîner sans péché chez les athées, ils se damnent tout seuls,' said the Abbé Jérôme Coignard. The Philosophy of Disillusion has nothing to offer save an entirely disinterested intellectual gratification. There are those to whom such a gratification is the most precious part of their experience, but they are very few, and such disinterested spectators of life cannot be either proselytisers or fanatics. They have no quarrel with life, they are far from the intellectual arrogance of pessimism; on the contrary, echoing Renan's 'Faisons le spectacle aussi varié que possible,' they wish, and, *au besoin*, encourage the Vital Instinct to work as energetically as is compatible with their own safety. But what of the other camp? Is it permissible, to put the question in the terms of M. de Gaultier's hypothesis, to attempt to anticipate the secret of Life, to prophesy the next mask which the Vital Instinct will assume? The masks of philosophical religion, (Protestantism filtering into Deism,) and humanitarian rationalism, seem torn past mending. It is difficult to imagine a new one. There is, of course, science, but, apart from experimentalists, it does not seem capable of creating any great enthusiasm. Its intellectual prestige, and its value for industrialism, for the improvement of the material conditions of life, leave untouched the emotional part of man's imagination. Under these circumstances it seems not impossible that the Vital Instinct may return to its earliest, most impenetrable mask, that of direct revelation. The means is at hand. In spite of philosophers, the Church is still in the world, and the principle of the Church is as irrefutable as it is indemonstrable. Its methods of representation will, no doubt, have to be modified, theology has been refuted as fact, and the shreds of philosophy with which its apologists have attempted to drape it have been ruthlessly torn from it. But surely neither the vital instinct nor the Church will be embarrassed by such trifles. It may be doubted whether any single human being has ever believed in a religious dogma as the conclusion of a syllogism. *Abyssus abyssum invocat.* The man in whom the vital instinct clamours for the satisfaction of religion has already a subconscious faith in religion. And the impossibility of establishing such faith either on external facts or on philosophy, when thoroughly brought home to him, leaves him with the alternative of acceptance of authority or despair. Between the two the Vital Instinct cannot hesitate. A certain kind of temperament is as much determined to believe in religion as a certain kind of intellect is determined to do without that belief. Or rather, to be exact, the difference is not between a temperament and an intellect, if, for the sake of argument, these convenient distinctions may be drawn, but between two kinds of temperament. Pascal had certainly as much intellect as ever fell to the lot of the most disabused philosopher. He himself indeed was one of the greatest of philosophic Nihilists,[1] but his intellect did not prevent him believing in the God of Jansenism. And this suggests another reflection. The psychological unity of the individual, except in a purely practical and relative sense, is a deduction from spiritualist philosophy. There is no scientific reason for thinking that a man's intellect and temperament must be unified. Experience also shows us that such unification is by no means necessary. Pascal is a case in point, and Gassendi was an excellent priest and an atheist in philosophy. Similarly, there seems no reason why a man should not accept the Philosophy of Disillusion with his intellect and the Church with his Vital Instinct. Such an attitude, to whatever other criticisms it

[1] I hope to discuss this elsewhere in detail.

may be open, at least, in no way offends the laws of the intelligence. It is an acute remark of M. de Gaultier's that if Kant had been a Catholic he would not have written the *Critique of Practical Reason.* Whether such an attitude is likely to be widespread is another matter. A man will hardly reach the conclusions of philosophic disillusion unless he is the fortunate or unfortunate possessor of an unusually developed instinct of knowledge. The use of his mind must have been a dominant and disinterested passion to him, bringing him its own joy, simply by its exercise and quite independently of its conclusions. An individual's energy being necessarily limited, it seems unlikely that the Vital Instinct will be strong enough to create the religious need in such a man. But the possibility of such a case cannot be denied either by science or by the Philosophy of Disillusion.

S. Domenico di Fiesole,
October 1908.